CHRISTMAS ISLAND

157°15′W

2°00′N

hristmas (Casady)
Airfield

N.E. Point

NANA

anulu
goon

Bay

of

Wrecks

Artemia

Joe's Hill (Collimes)

les

'A' Site

Site

Aeon Point

Aeon Airfield

S.E.
Point

Korean
Wreck

THE CHRISTMAS ISLAND STORY

Eric Bailey

STACEY INTERNATIONAL

ISBN 0 905743 08 3

First published by Stacey International 1977
© The Gilbert Islands Government·

Stacey International
128 Kensington Church Street
London w8 4BH
Set in Monotype Bembo and printed by
Willsons Printers (Leicester) Ltd

Design: Anthony Nelthorpe MSIAD

CONTENTS

ILLUSTRATIONS

Inside front cover
Map of Christmas Island

*To the people of
the Gilbert Islands*

ABAKIRORO
The Far-away Island

There were not the fmalleft traces of any human being having ever been here before us; and, indeed, fhould any one be fo unfortunate as to be accidentally driven upon the ifland, or left there, it is hard to fay, that he could be able to prolong exiftence. There is, indeed, abundance of birds and fifh; but no vifible means of allaying thirft, nor any vegetable that could fupply the place of bread, or correct the bad effects of an animal diet; which, in all probability, would foon prove fatal alone.

Reproduction from *A Voyage to the Pacific Ocean* 1784

THUS THE verdict of Captain James Cook, writing in his Journal in the great cabin of Her Majesty's ship *Resolution* as she sailed away from Christmas Island on the 2nd January, 1778. There were in fact many after him who were "driven upon the island, or left there" and survived, albeit not without hardship. There were indeed also some traces of earlier human habitation and his First Lieutenant, John Gore, records in his log:

11

"No inhabitants nor signs of any. Some of our people indeed saw some Round Stones round which there lay broken shells. They likewise saw some cleared places such as where they thought huts had been."

Cook was not alone in his dismal view of Christmas Island, which seems to have led a sort of see-saw existence of favour and abandonment in the field of human endeavour and occupation. A later owner, Father Emmanuel Rougier, was almost lyrical in his account of the island after his first view in 1912: "no difficulty in getting fresh water for drinking in any place: seven thousand bearing coconut trees and ten thousand non-bearing: guano or phosphates are a by-product: millions and millions of birds and something can be done in that line" and later registering his company stated "the intention is to populate the island with colonists and workers of all nationalities and colours".

H. E. Maude, when Commissioner of Lands for the Gilbert and Ellice Islands, to which colonial group Christmas Island was attached in July 1919, was another enthusiast who at first acquaintance thought that three-quarters of the island's 140 square miles of land could be planted to coconuts, that sheep and even cattle could graze "on the plains of waving green grass" and that it would absorb some eight thousand settlers from the crowded Gilbert Islands. He believed then that the island was drought free, but Phil. F. D. Palmer, Manager of nearby Fanning Island, who visited on the same occasion, saw much evidence of palms "with severe constriction of the trunks extending several feet, followed by bulges," from which he deduced that the normal state on the island was one of drought punctuated only by short periods of heavy rainfall and subsequent rapid growth. He recommended his employers against purchase and those who read the two reports found it difficult to believe that they were written about the same island at the same time.

Christmas Island is indeed subject to severe and sometimes prolonged drought and no doubt Captain Cook's visit coincided with one of these. The average rainfall is about thirty inches annually and in the last twenty-five years there are only eleven years on which this has been reached or exceeded, four of them since 1972. No doubt this climatic inhospitability was a factor which determined that there should never have been a permanent indigenous habitation. But other forces of which nothing is known were at work, for none of the Line Islands, north or south of the Equator, had a native population and certainly Fanning Island, 150 miles to the north of Christmas, is both accessible and fertile.

That there have been periodic occupations is well established by the archaeological remains which have been found and were exhaustively investigated by the "Kaimiloa" expedition of the Bernice P. Bishop Museum of Hawaii in 1924. Kenneth P. Emory of the Museum and leader of the expedition summarizes the results of his visit to Christmas Island:

"Christmas Island has not so far yielded definite evidence of settlement by Polynesians. The two sites which might have been villages have yielded no artifacts—an indication of temporary occupation. Though a number of structures have been found which might have been simple platform maraes, it is not possible to prove they are maraes. The few scattered traces of early Polynesian visitors or castaways are the coconut groves, basalt adze, shell adze, petroglyph, coral mounds and platforms, and burials. The basalt adze was certainly from some volcanic island. If its form is as Rougier remembered it, it probably came from western Polynesia. The shell adze is of a type, common in Micronesia and the Ellice Islands, which appears as far east as Pukapuka and Tongareva. The petroglyphs are Polynesian. Although their form is too generalized to make it possible to associate them with a definite area, it can be seen that they resemble Hawaiian rather than Tahitian petroglyphs. The simple coral mounds, surmounted by an upright stone, the cist burial, and the simple burial are all difficult to assign to any particular source. Evidently these traces of Polynesian visitors or castaways belong to quite different periods and come from quite different directions."

Why they came and why they went is a parenthesis of stepping stones in the wider mystery of the great Polynesian triangle from New Zealand to the Marquesas and northward to Hawaii. It is generally accepted that Hawaii was settled from the Marquesas but that would take voyagers far to the east of the Line Islands. A return trip to Tahiti, however, would find more favourable winds on a route which would lie close to Fanning and Christmas Islands.

An hypothesis which found favour with anthropologists thirty years ago suggests that these ancient voyagers followed the migratory paths of land birds, knowing from observation year after year that, as they could not land on the sea, they must be flying to land elsewhere. The Golden Plover migrates south from Alaska in the northern winter to Tahiti, passes through Hawaii and rests on other islands en route and some authorities believe that it was deliberately followed by adventurers. Today there seems to be a leaning rather to the theory that the birds were followed perforce by those who were driven from their homes or otherwise found themselves in unknown seas.

However that may be, land birds certainly use the Line Islands and a former District Officer on Fanning Island writes of his personal experience in 1939 when he "stood on the shore of the island and watched birds flying in from the north. Some crashed in the sea; others just made it to the beach. The latter were totally exhausted and often little more than skin and bones. They did not offer—indeed, they could not offer—any resistance to being picked up and examined. They would stay for two or three weeks on the island resting and recuperating before once more winging their way south".

H.M.S. Gannet which visited Christmas Island in 1881 included a note in the Remarks Book that:

> "Wild duck were plentiful, but in October were in very poor condition and could be knocked over with sticks; we were told they had just arrived and were thin and exhausted after their long flight from California."

Christmas Island has been almost continuously occupied only since 1882, when the first attempt was made to plant coconuts for copra production commercially. But even in that comparatively short period it has drawn its workers from Hawaii,

Manahiki, Tahiti, Niue and, since 1941, from the Gilbert and Ellice Islands, although Gilbertese were working in Fanning and Washington nearly fifty years before that. The owners have included New Zealanders, British and Tahitians, and there have also been military incursions by both American and British forces.

The names which are found on the map of Christmas Island today are a reflection of its recent polyglot history: "Cook Island"; the appropriately named "Bay of Wrecks", "Aeon Point" recording a 5,000 ton timber ship which came to grief on 18th July, 1908; "Benson Point" for a shipwrecked Captain who spent seven months on the island with his crew in 1836; "Greig's Grove" for the owner of Fanning Island who made trial plantings in 1880; "Paris" where the French owner lived, and naturally across the "channel"—"London", and also "Collimes", "Auverne", "Le Bourget" and "Algeria"; "New Zealand Airfield" surveyed but never built; "Casady Airfield" for the young American pilot of the 12th Pursuit Squadron, who failed to return from an alert patrol on 23rd March, 1942; "Main Camp", "Decca Waterhole"; "Banana", "A" Site and "M" Site from the days of the British atomic tests; "Artemia" the scientific name for the brine shrimp, the hope for a new industry; "NASDA" for the down-range tracking station of the National Space Development Agency of Japan; "Motu Tabu", a "restricted island" in the lagoon from the Polynesian and Gilbertese, who have also their own name for Christmas Island—*Abakiroro*—The Faraway Island.

CAPTAIN JAMES COOK

CAPTAIN COOK's ten day association with Christmas Island was casual and practical. He received from it a good supply of fresh meat in the shape of 300 turtles and a firm base to observe an eclipse of the sun. He gave in return a name and a fixed location for the chart-makers. On this, the Third Voyage to the Pacific, the main purpose was no longer the exploration of the islands of the South Seas and his previous ten months, spent largely in Tonga and on a fifth visit to Tahiti and the Society Islands, had been devoted less to the pursuit of "Geography and Navigation" than to a more mature observation of Polynesian society.

He was nearly three months in the Tongan Islands, but did not follow, as he would have done on the previous voyages, clear leads which pointed to major land groups at Fiji and Samoa, both within comfortable sailing distance in the time available. Christmas Island, as the chart reproduced in his Journal shows, received a fairly cursory survey of its western bay where the ships anchored and little indication of its real

17

shape and size. No doubt he had seen too many such "low islands so common in this ocean; that is, a narrow bank of land inclosing the sea within" and this a not particularly inviting one, where "a few cocoa-nut trees were seen in two or three places; but, in general, the land had a very barren appearance".

How Cook came to be in the Pacific at all as Post Captain in command of two Naval ships, the *Resolution* of 462 tons and the *Discovery* of 298 tons, is itself a remarkable story of merit recognised and rewarded. Born in a small farming community in north Yorkshire on 27th October, 1728, the second son of an immigrant Scots farm labourer and his English wife, he was fortunate to have some writing, reading, arithmetic and his catechism at the village school. Thus equipped, he became at seventeen shop boy to a grocer and haberdasher at the fishing port of Staithes. Here perhaps he first felt the lure of the sea, for eighteen months later he was bound "apprentice and servant" to John Walker, Quaker shipmaster in Whitby engaged in the coal trade, which in those days employed 1000 ships on the east coast of England. On 20th April, 1750 Cook appears in a ship's muster roll as a "seaman" for the first time and he continued to sail the North Sea in Walker's ships as far as Norway, with several voyages to Ireland transferring military troops and their horses from Holland. "Mate" in 1752, he was offered his own ship as "Master" in 1755 at the age of 27. To everybody's amazement he declined and on 17th June, volunteered into the Royal Navy as an able seaman.

He remained, however, a life-long friend of John Walker and all of the ships with which he went exploring — the *Endeavour* of the First Voyage, the *Resolution*, the *Adventure* and the *Discovery* of the Second and Third Voyages were "cats" built in the Whitby shipyards and bought by the Admiralty out of the coal trade for their strength, capacity and ability to take the ground.

Sent to H.M.S. *Eagle*, a 60-gun ship, his previous experience was recognised by Captain Hugh Palliser and within a month he was appointed Master's Mate. Two years later, after service on the blockade of the French coast, he passed his examination as "Master". The Master of a Naval ship in those days was not an officer, but had great responsibility as the principal navigator with special responsibilities for pilotage, harbour work and charting, as well as overseeing the masts, yards, sails and rigging. In the 1250-ton *Pembroke* he was soon on his way to the war with the French in Canada and was present at the fall of Quebec. It was, however, his subsequent work from 1763–67, charting and surveying the southern and western coasts of Newfoundland with a skill and determination which caused those working seventy and a hundred years later over the same ground to say that only two of their predecessors could be trusted, "Cook and Lane" (then Cook's assistant), that made him known to the Admiralty and the Royal Society. Thus came his appointment as Lieutenant to command an expedition to the South Seas to carry a scientific party to observe the Transit of Venus. This phenomenon, occurring only twice every hundred years, when recorded at different parts of the earth's surface would determine for the first time the distance of the Earth from the Sun and give a unit of measurement of the universe itself. The observation of eclipses, like that on Christmas Island, was an opportunity never missed by Cook as a means of verifying longitude, the determination of which was only just becoming a practical possibility.

There was indeed a Board of Longitude in England which offered a prize of £20,000 to anyone who could produce a "generally practicable and useful method" of fixing longitude at sea "within thirty miles at the end of a six week's voyage". By the end of his First Voyage Cook had become expert and devotee of the lunar method which enabled him to map the coasts of both north and south islands of New Zealand and eastern Australia with an accuracy which remains valid to this day. On his Second Voyage he set out with some scepticism to test the effectiveness of four chronometers, but by its end was to express his faith in "Mr. Kendall's watch machine" which accompanied him later to Christmas Island and remained in naval service until 1802.

The determination of longitude was one of the important subsidiary tasks of the Second Voyage, of which the purpose was to discover or disprove the great southern continent which geographers and philosophers were sure must exist to "balance" the land masses of the northern hemisphere. In this quest he spent two southern summers on the first ice-edge navigation, which took him three times across the Antarctic Circle. That he spent two Christmas Days amongst the icebergs was perhaps fortunate in inhibiting a further proliferation of places named "Christmas". On the First Voyage Cook spent his Christmases in the Atlantic, off the north cape of New Zealand and in Batavia. On the second voyage he gave the name "Christmas Sound" to an anchorage near Cape Horn and outward bound on the Third Voyage he named a "Christmas Harbour" on ice-bound Kerguelen Island, far south of the Indian Ocean, but both have acquired other names in the intervening centuries. Only "Christmas Island" in the Indian Ocean today plagues Cook's "Christmas Island" with misdirected mail, and for that a Captain Wm. Mynors of the East India Company, who sighted and named it in 1643, was responsible!

The purpose of the Third Voyage was to settle another famous controversy which had inspired some fifty previous expeditions—the "North-West Passage" round the north of the American continent to give a quick route from Europe to the Pacific and the Indies and incidentally to outwit the Spaniards, who still protested a jealous but weakening claim to the Pacific, across which they had journeyed for 200 years, between Acapulco and the Philippines.

It is somewhat surprising that in all that time they had not become acquainted with the north-south string of the Line Islands or the Hawaiian archipelago. But the inability to determine longitude made it customary for mariners to make for the latitude of their destination and then sail along it until they arrived. The Spaniards sailed west with the easterly trades just south of the Equator and returned with the westerlies in the northern forties, north of Hawaii.

When therefore Cook set sail on 9th December, 1777 on his way to Drake's "New Albion" on the American coast—today's California—he was able to write in his Journal:

"Before I sailed from the Society Islands, I lost no opportunity of inquiring of the inhabitants, if there were any islands in a north or north-west direction from them, but I did not find that they know of any."

This argues a substantial break in tradition, for it is certain that there had been contact in earlier centuries which carried the Polynesians to Hawaii and left traces of temporary occupation on the intervening islands.

Unknown to Cook there had also been one Spanish sighting of Christmas Island in about the year 1537. Cortez, conqueror of Mexico, had sent one of his captains, Hernando de Grijalva, to explore the eastern Pacific for some rich islands rumoured to lie to the west of the Americas. Abandoning his search he tried to return, but was constantly driven back by East and North-east winds. When again near the Equator the crew demanded that Grijalva should make before the wind for the Moluccas. On his refusal they killed him and sailed due west. Wrecked on the northern coast of New Guinea the seven survivors were sold as slaves and some were later ransomed by Antonio Galvano, Portuguese Governor of the Moluccas who recorded their story; although he did not believe it, for he was sure they had been sent by Cortez in search of "the Islands of Cloves". One of these islands he described as being "above a thousand leagues without the sight of land, on the one side nor yet on the other of the equinoctiall. And in two degrees toward the north they discovered one island named Acea". Despite the absence of any description of "Acea" there is said to be little difficulty in identifying it as Christmas Island, there being no other land which could be thus located. Although there is no clue to the origin of the name "Acea", it is presumed to have been bestowed by the Spanish mariners who appear neither to have landed nor spoken to any inhabitants.

Cook sailed due north from Borabora, making some westing due to winds and currents, and relying on those westerly winds which carried the Spaniards back to Mexico to take him too to the west coast of America. His instructions were to make a landfall at Latitude 45°, today's Oregon, in order not further to alarm the Spaniards: the *Resolution*'s first suggested name *Drake* had been changed for the same reason. The Spanish Court saw no scientific justification for the voyage and had sent orders to the Viceroy of Mexico "to seize and imprison him if possible".

From 16th December, 1777, he began to record sighting of birds "such as boobies, tropic and men-of-war birds, tern and some other sorts". He was undoubtedly close to flat sandy Starbuck, but saw nothing until, just after daybreak on 24th, they came in sight of Christmas Island to the north-east. The ship made a few "boards" to get into the lee of the western coast and dropped anchor on a sandy bottom in thirty fathoms of water. The sea "broke in a dreadful surf all along the shore" as it does today, and it was left until the next morning to make an accurate survey for a landing. Two boats were sent on this duty and two others to fish at a grappling from the shore, the first survey the previous day having reported an abundance of fish, also happily still true today. These boats were back for breakfast with "upward of two hundred weight of fish".

At noon the Master of *Resolution*, William Bligh—then aged twenty-two, but in later life to become a public and controversial figure as Captain of the *Bounty* and Governor of the Colony of New South Wales—reported a channel into the lagoon to the north, though only fit for boats. This was, how-ever, a landing-place and in consequence the "ships weighed anchor and after two or three trips, came to again in twenty fathoms of water over a bottom of fine dark sand, before a small island that lies at the entrance to the lagoon". This island, on which Cook, King, the Second Lieutenant with astronomical training, and Bayly, astronomer, watched the eclipse on 1st January, 1778—and therefore called by King "Eclipse Island" —is now known as "Cook Island" and is a bird sanctuary.

The following day the turtle hunt began in earnest and parties remained ashore for the purpose for the rest of the stay. At first the turtles were carried from the ocean beaches across the island to the lagoon, but after two days Lieutenant William-son found a landing place in what is now known as Vaskess Bay, just east of the South-West Point, and the boats were sent round by sea to collect turtles there. It was, however, during this duty of carrying the turtles to the boats that two seamen lost their way. Disagreeing about the most probable track to bring them back to their companions, they had separated. Cook recorded of one man,

"In order to allay his thirst, he had recourse to the singular expedient of killing turtles, and drinking their blood. His mode of refreshing himself, when weary, of which he said he felt the good effects, was equally whimsical. He undressed himself, and lay down for sometime in the shallow water upon the beach."

This man after twenty-four hours absence was described as being "in great distress", but his companion was another day missing, and according to the log of John Williamson, Third Lieutenant in the *Resolution*, they

"found him almost dead. He has several times tried to drink the blood of birds—["they were so tame that you might take them with your hands" reported Bayly]—and even his own urine, but could not swallow either and having met with a pool of clear water he went into it with his clothes on in hope of refreshing himself, but unluckily this water to which he had been invited by its transparancy proved no other than a pool of strong brine, by which his limbs and clothes become so stiff that he was hardly able to crawl out and in this condition he was found."

Writing of these brine ponds, which are still a feature of Christmas Island, Cook comments that one of the lost men found some salt on the South-east part of the island.

"But, though this was a article of which we were in want, a man who could lose himself, as he did, and not know whether he was travelling, East, West, North or South, was not to be depended upon as a fit guide to conduct us to the place. . . . It was a surprise to everyone how these two men could contrive to lose themselves. The land not more than three miles across, flat with a few shrubs scattered upon it; and, from many parts of it, the masts of the ships could easily be seen. But this was a rule of direction they never once thought of; nor did they recollect in what quarter of the island the ships had anchored; and they were as much at a loss how to get back to them, or to the party they had straggled from, as if they had but just dropped from the clouds. Considering how strange a set of beings the generality of seamen are, when on shore, instead of being surprised that these two men should thus lose their way, it is rather to be wondered at, that no more of the party were missing."

Although it is clear that Cook was on Christmas Island at a time of severe drought and vegetation was perhaps particularly sparse, the master of navigation underestimates the very real difficulties for ordinary mortals of orientation on a large island absolutely flat. Scrub, only the height of a man, cuts off any distant view and the slant of the equatorial sun gives little indication of direction except early in the morning and in the late afternoon. Those who live on Christmas Island today have not been without experience of losing themselves even where they felt themselves on familiar ground, but could locate no landmark nor follow a straight path among the numerous small lagoons.

An American from Groton, Connecticut, John Ledyard, was serving in *Resolution* as a Corporal of Marines. In later years he was to enter folk legend when he set out to walk across Siberia and the American continent and died on his way to look for the sources of the Niger. He wrote an account of his service with Cook and made the tale of the missing seamen one of the highlights of the voyage. With an astonishing use of imagination he furnished Christmas Island with deserts, forests, mountains and ferocious animals!

Even in the absence of such hindrances, hauling the turtles across a mile or two of sharp coral fragments and sand must indeed have been gruelling work, especially when, according to Thomas Edgar, Master in the *Discovery* — "The largest weighed 132 lbs and the smallest not less than 40 or 50 lbs" and little wonder that Lieutenant Williamson reported his men as "having every part of them that was exposed to the sun scorched and blistered".

But all was not drudgery for these turtle hunters, as the young Cornish Midshipman, James Trevenen, was to chronicle

24

in his log, and had something to add too regarding the dangers
of the passage into the lagoon and the abundance of shark:

"I had this boat to bring off turtle in all the time of our stay here
and the service was a rather perilous one, for we had to pull into
the lagoon over a very high sea (which, however, never broke)
through a narrow passage with which we were little acquainted
and where we could see the bottom under us the whole way;
had any sunken rock projected up a little higher than the rest we
would have been destroyed, but luckily we never encountered
any. On every side of us swam Sharks innumerable and so
voracious that they bit our oars and rudder and I actually struck my
hanger two inches into the back of one whilst he had the
rudder between his teeth. The boats fishing for Cavallies
and etc. in Shallow water, carried long pikes to keep the Sharks
from the Bait. On board the Ships the Sailors caught great
numbers, and as these two beings are at constant war with each
other, contrived a hundred ways to torment them, sometimes two
were firmly lashed together by the Tails and turned adrift—
others had large pieces of board tied under their heads, This is
called Spritsail yarding them, and hinders them from sinking, so
that we saw them floating and vainly attempting to dive, as far as
the eye could reach. Besides turning the Turtle on their backs
when they are asleep (the common way of catching them) we
took them another way, which offered us great sport. On the
Tides subsiding there remained no more than a foot of water
(more or less) on the reef, which extend half a mile from the
shore, where it was bounded by a higher ridge, but there were
many very deep holes in which the Turtles used to remain till
the rising of the water again. The water was so clear that we
could see them in these, and as all our people swim to perfection,
they would dive down and either catch them by the Fins or put
them out and then the chase and sport began. We as well as the
Turtles dashed through thick and thin and very many ludicrous
scenes occurred. In deep water they had the advantage, but
when there was not more than six inches we would come up
with them and catch them by the Fins, but as often one was not
strong enough to hold them, he would be dragged along,
sometimes up, sometimes down, till others came to his
assistance, on meeting a large pool through which he must be

dragged head foremost, perhaps the Turtle would escape and I have seen one, larger than common, thus taken three times and at last escape throu' a passage in the reef into the open Sea. This chase was chequered with all the vicissitudes of hope and fear that can enliven any other and was surely equally interesting, and more so as perhaps our dinner depended on it. In this manner we once caught forty-two in half an hour."

The Christmas Island passage, whilst normally easy of access, still has its variable moods, and strong westerly swells from distant storm centres can—even on otherwise calm and windless days—build up heavy surf, sometimes breaking all across from Cook Island to London. At its most spectacular, the strong easterly wind blowing into the face of the incoming swell causes the breakers on Cockrane Reef to rear up almost perpendicular and plucks the foam from the crest in a feathery plume laid out to the west. The sharks too have not deserted the island as many a fisherman has discovered, ruefully hauling in the cleanly severed head of tuna; but there is no record or remembrance of any attack upon a human.

The turtle—in Cook's words "they were all of the green kind; and perhaps as good as any in the world"—is now a rarity upon the island. Perhaps Cook's report of his success with them led too many ships to seek fresh meat here. The "people" of the *Resolution* and *Discovery* had fresh pork for their Christmas dinner on 26th December, but turtle became their staple thereafter until reaching the Hawaiian Islands on 20th January.

A fresh food diet was almost a passion with Cook, who was one of the first sea captains to defeat the killing disease of scurvy. In these days it may not seem so large an achievement to have arrived at Batavia with only three men sick after two years and two months at sea on the First Voyage (he was to lose seven men from malaria contracted in Java and a further twenty-three from the "bloody flux"—dysentery—after he sailed), or after the Second Voyage to report to the Admiralty: "having been absent from England Three Years and Eighteen Days, in which time I lost but four men and only one of them by sickness". But the exceptional nature of this record can be understood when compared with that of two Dutch East Indiamen who arrived at Cape Town, outward bound, a few days after Cook and had "between them since leaving Europe lost almost two hundred men".

Cook's regimen, we learn from the logs, included having the bilge pumped out regularly with fresh sea water, the ship cleaned, aired and dried with charcoal fires; the brewing of Pelham's "experimental beer", the men compelled to air their bedding, to wash and dry their clothes properly and frequently. He was willing to experiment with any hopeful suggestion — salted cabbage in addition to sauerkraut, on which he placed much reliance, extra wheat, portable soup-cakes of a sort of glue or meat essence, a boiled down syrup of oranges and lemons, oatmeal, Baron Storch's marmalade of yellow carrots. But before all came his insistence upon fresh food wherever and whenever it could be obtained. Early on the First Voyage a sailor and a marine who refused their allowance of fresh beef were deemed guilty of mutiny and given a dozen lashes each.

This was the only occasion on which Cook used corporal punishment as a persuader and later we find him adopting the expedient of having new items of diet dressed for the Captain and the officers and leaving it to the option of the men:

> "for such are the Tempers and dispositions of Seamen in general that whatever you give them out of the Common way although it be ever so much for their good, yet it will not go down with them and you will hear nothing but murmurings gainst the man that first invented it; but the Moment they see their Superiors set a Value upon it, it becomes the finest stuff in the world and the inventor a damn'd honest fellow."

These seamen were not, however, so witless as not to profit by their Captain's obsession and would secure his favourable opinion by coming aboard ostentatiously bearing a bunch of greens plucked ashore!

Quite apart from the problems of diet, the cramped conditions in which the ship's company lived is itself almost a miracle of survival. With a three-years' voyage before them the ships carried a mass of spare canvas, rope and spars, powder and shot for the guns—twelve four-pounders, twelve swivel guns and twelve musquetoons for the *Resolution* and eight of each for the *Discovery*, two small vessels in frame to be put together at need, several tons of iron and coal in ballast. And then oil and vinegar, barrels of salt beef, salt pork, salt fat, hard-baked "bread", dried pease and the daily issue of spirits for the men, 3,032 gallons of Madeira wine for the officers and clothing for 112 in the *Resolution* and seventy in the *Discovery*. Then the supernumeraries, a Pacific Islander to be returned home with the baggage and gifts bestowed upon him—including a suit of armour!—a landscape painter, an astronomer and a botanist with their gear and collections. In addition to a large supply of "trade goods", the *Resolution* carried from England sheep, goats, pigs, rabbits, turkeys, geese, ducks and chickens, a bull, two cows and their calves and a peacock and hen with forage for their sustenance. At Cape Town Cook added considerably to all varieties of stock including another bull and heifers and four horses and he wrote to Lord Sandwich, First Lord of the Admiralty: "nothing is wanting but a few females of our own species to make the *Resolution* a compleate ark". These animals were for the improvement of the islands' stock, though as much to provide fresh provender for visiting ships as for local consumption.

Before he arrived at Christmas Island all the animals had been given to Chiefs of the islands from Tasmania and New Zealand to Tonga, Tahiti and her neighbours. But Cook was able to leave something:

> "having some cocoa-nuts and yams on board, in a state of vegitation, I ordered them to be planted on the little island where we observed the eclipse; and some melon seeds were sown in another place."

He also left a bottle to the honour of George III recording the visit of the two ships. Fortunately his ships were anchored too far from the shore to enable him to attempt an expedient adopted at Morea and Raiatea of building a wooden gangway from ship to shore in the hope of inducing some of his superfluity of rats to take advantage of it. To this day Christmas

Island remains free of the European ship rat, the scourge of the coconut, and the mouse-like Polynesian rat, found by Cook, remains alone, although it has since acquired a predator in the domestic cat, which has gone wild and can be seen anywhere in the island.

So Cook sailed away from the islet, which now bears his name and which he observed "lies in the latitude 1° 59' North, and in the longitude of 202° 30' East, determined by a considerable number of lunar observations, which differed only 7' from the time-keeper; it being so much less". And, as elsewhere, where Cook said it was, so it is today—157° 30' West—a facet of the professionalism of this incredible man, which was to draw away from the high-spirited Trevenen—who called him "despot" in another context—a tribute to "the sublime and soaring genius of a Cook".

Eighteen days out from Christmas Island, Cook made one of his major discoveries, the Sandwich Islands—Hawaii. He stayed but three days on the island of Kauai for he needed to reach the high latitudes to the north in early summer. After another outstanding survey of the Canadian west coast and of south and west Alaska he passed the Arctic Circle on 17th August, 1778, searched the edge of the ice from the north Alaskan coast to Siberia and finally disposed of the myth of a navigable northwest passage.

A month later he sailed south and by Christmas Day was off the island of Owhyhe, where he planned to spend the winter charting. On 17th January, 1779, he landed at Kealakekua Bay on the west coast and was received in a manner which has led many to believe that he was identified with the benevolent demi-god of Hawaiian mythology, Lono. On the 4th February he sailed north, but a violent storm sprung his foremast and he was forced to return to Kealakekua. There he was to find that sudden change in the reaction of the people to both himself and his ships, which led to a tragic accumulation of misunderstandings, culminating in his violent death at the water's edge on 13th February, 1779.

THE NINETEENTH CENTURY

THE GEOGRAPHICAL framework of the Pacific was now firmly established and in the wake of Cook came some who had served with him, Bligh and Vancouver, Midshipman in the *Resolution*; other British Naval Captains—Byron, Fearne, FitzRoy and Gilbert; Americans, Fanning and Mackay and the French. And after them the nineteenth-century merchant adventurers in search of whale-oil, whale-bone for women's corsets, phosphate-guano to stimulate the soils of Europe and America to feed the rapidly expanding urban populations, mother-of-pearl for buttons, coconut-oil, labour for Australian and Hawaiian plantations and the mines of Peru. The metropolitan powers too, at first obliged to look to the interests and excesses of their nationals, eventually identified their own needs in an expansionist era and took steps to secure harbours and coaling stations for their ships and in the Line Islands a mid-way station for a submarine cable to stretch a third of the way around the globe's circumference from Canada to Australia and New

Zealand. Two ships of the Royal Navy followed Cook to Christmas Island, *H.M.S. Samarang* on 11th September, 1840 and *H.M.S. Reindeer* (the whim perhaps of some humorist in the British Admiralty) on 11th-12th June, 1868 and in the last twenty years of the century, eight more.

That whalers and shark-fishers from Hawaii were using Christmas Island as a source of "turtle, fish and cocoa-nuts" is learnt from F. D. Bennett, who was the first after Cook to publish an account of a visit, which lasted several days, by the British whaler *Tuscan* in May 1835. He made his way round more than two-thirds of the coast and found the island to be uninhabited and that the yams, melons and coconuts planted by Cook, and the bottle left to commemorate the discovery, had all disappeared. More than fifty coconut trees had been felled by previous visitors, who had recorded the names of their ships on the surviving trees. One of these was a Capt. W. T. Brooks of England, who recorded in his log that he had taken on supplies in 1829, and the first-known American visitor, John Stetson of New Haven, Connecticut, reported landing from the ship *Equator* at about this period.

On 10th October, 1836 shortly after Bennett's visit, the English whaling ship *Briton* became the first known victim of the treacherous Bay of Wrecks. Captain George Benson and his crew were to spend more than seven months on the island before being taken off by the American whaler *Charles Frederic* on 23rd May, 1837. Captain Benson, a man of energy and enterprise, occupied himself in exploring, charting, digging wells and planting coconuts as landmarks. The ship's surgeon, one F. H. Tresilian, in his account, remarks, of the trees cut down in the grove by the southern entrance to the lagoon, that "a number of ships have been there and a variety of English and American ships' names were marked on them, but none were dated later than 1834".

Both Bennett and Benson felt that Cook had greatly under-estimated the size of the island and the number of coconut trees — Benson estimating about 2,000 in several clumps. To Cook the island:

An engraving of
Captain James Cook
published in April 1799
by I. K. Sherwin from a
painting by N. Dance.

i

1778
Jan.ʸ 7

bird like a hedge sparrow; land crabs, small lizards and rats. The land is in some places produceth a few shrubs and plants, the soil here is light and black, evidently compased of decayed vegetables, and the dung of birds and sand. There are other places again, where nothing but marine productions, such as broken coral stones, shells &c.ᵃ are to be seen; These are thrown up in long narrow ridges, lying in a paralel direction with the sea coast, not unlike a ploughed field, and must have been done by the sea though at this time it does not reach some of these places by a mile or more. This is, I think, an incontestable proof that this island has been produced by marine productions and is in a state of increase; for not only the broken coral, but the shells are many of them too large and too heavy for any bird to bury from the seacoast to where they now lay. Not a drop of fresh water was any where found though dug for in several places; there were several ponds of salt water in the land and one of the last men found some salt, on the S.ᵉ part of the island; this was an article we were in want of, but a man who could lose himself as he did, and not know whether he was travelling East, West, North or South, was not to be depended upon to find the place.

As we kept our Christmas here I called it Christmas Island, I judge it to be about fifteen or twenty leagues in circuit; it seemed to be of a semicircular form, or like the Moon in the last quarter, the two horns being the north and south points, and bear from each other, nearly N.b.E and S.b.W. four or five leagues distant. This West side, or the isle at the entrance into the lagoon on which we observed the Eclipse, lies in the Latitude of 1°.59′ — ″ North, and

Above: *an extract from
Cook's journal for
January 1778.*

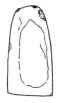

*Artifacts found at
Christmas Island.
Left: a petroglyph.
Far left: a Tridacna
shell adz. Length 3ins,
width of cutting edge
1.5ins, thickness
0.5ins, weight 2.5ozs.*

Bottom left: *Larcum Kendall's Timekeeper (1769) used by Captain Cook on both his Second and Third Voyages.*

The Discovery *(298 tons) was the smaller of the two ships Cook took on his Second (1772–75) and Third (1776–80) Voyages.*

Above: *intensive hunting has made the turtle a rarity on the island.*

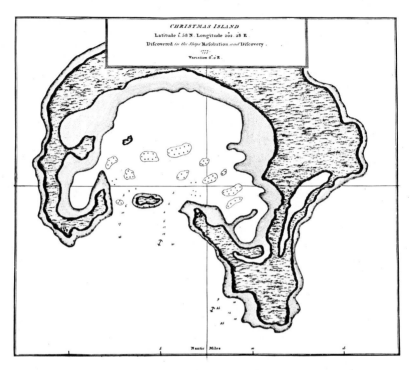

CHRISTMAS ISLAND
Latitude 1.58 N. Longitude 202.28 E.
Discovered in the Ships Resolution and Discovery.
1777
Variation 6°.0 E.

Nautic Miles

iv

Above: *a local stamp for Christmas Island issued by Fr. Rougier. This stamp is of the Third Issue when the value was changed from five cents to ten in 1926. The stamps were used for letters and packets carried in the Company's vessels from Christmas Island.*

Above left: *a map of Christmas Island charted by Captain James Cook in 1777.*

Left: *whaling in the Pacific circa 1848.*

Right: *Rev. Father Petrics Emmanuel Rougier.*

Wharf   Diesel crane   Jetties   Copra b

Above: *a contemporary photograph of the wharf at London in 1949 taken from a coral patch at low tide, eight months after the departure of the American Forces which built the wharf during World War II.*

Right: *the Korean tuna-fishing vessel* Dai Ho No5 *ran on to the reef a few miles west of South East Point on 3rd March 1976, the last of the Christmas Island wrecks.*

ooden stage

Derelict buildings

Left: *an abandoned pier on the site of the military camp at the Lagoon's edge.*

Overleaf: *Britain's first nuclear test explosion at Christmas Island took place on 15th May 1957.*

"seemed to be of a semicircular form: or like the moon in the last quarter ... I judge it be about fifteen or twenty leagues in circumference."

As Lieutenant Williamson noted in his log: "from east to west we know little of it" and in fact an unusual arm of land fifteen miles in length and some four to five in breadth projects from the south-east corner and accounts for thirty miles of the total actual circumference of ninety-one miles. Thus, within the limits of his observation, Captain Cook is again shown to have been close in his judgement. "An Approximate Survey" made by Captain Scott of *H.M.S. Samarang* more than sixty years after Cook is by contrast wildly inaccurate and even the longitude is at fault. Some have also thought it impossible that the number of trees should have increased from the "thirty" which he reported to the two thousand found by Benson fifty-eight years later. It is significant, however, that the locations of palms indicated on Cook's sketch-map are all at places where normally the ground water is readily available and a few consecutive seasons of good rains can produce a rapid generation of fallen nuts.

The low-lying nature of the island, coupled with the strong inshore set of the current, especially in the north-eastern bight, led to many wrecks besides that of the *Briton*. Among those recorded was one which yielded the prow of a canoe and a mast terminating in a crescent; the Bremen whaler *Mozart*, laden with 4,000 barrels of oil and a considerable quantity of whalebone, was fortunate in being in the company of an American whaler, the *J. E. Donnell*; but the passengers and crew of the *Maria Helena*, a Chilean merchantman, wrecked less than a month later, had to remain on the island from 5th January until 16th March, 1848, before being rescued by the French sloop *Sarcelle*. A United States Government chart of the island dated 1874 bears within the Bay this note: "This bight is very dangerous. A vessel getting into it at night will have a small chance for getting out after discovering the breakers".

The year 1848 seems to have been a busy one for Christmas Island, which was also visited on 10th July by the trading vessel

33

Fairy belonging to the British firm of Collie and Lucette, based in Tahiti. Lucette, the owner, was on board. Five days later he landed at Fanning Island to set up a coconut oil establishment. On Fanning he found that some months before his arrival:

> "A man of Crusoe habits had taken up his abode there with his family and, isolated from the rest of the world, had devoted himself to the rearing of pigs, depending on the chance call of any whaler for a supply of those necessities which his habits of civilisation had rendered indispensable . . . His wife is a Kanaka woman of the Sandwich Islands, and he has a large family of children and grand-children."

This was John English, after whom "English Harbour" on Fanning Island is named and who appears to have become the Manager and later part-owner of the oil business in association with a Scotsman from Ayr, William Greig, and an American, George Bicknell, both of whom died on the island after long and full lives. Only the descendants of Greig carried on until financial problems and disputes with other shareholders caused them to sell out in 1907 to Father Emmanual Rougier, who plays a large part in the later Christmas Island story. The Fanning operation extended to Washington in about 1860 and sometime about 1880–81 an attempt was made to establish a plantation on Christmas Island. Although abandoned, "Greig's Grove" retains its name to this day and the Greig family name still flourishes in the Gilbert Islands.

Meanwhile, however, guano was the prize and the millions of birds which then, as now, invest Christmas Island led many to believe that it must be a rich source of the valuable fertilizer. Whether the large area of the island or some other environmental feature was responsible, the fact remains that the expectations were disappointed and guano was never extracted as a commercial proposition from Christmas Island.

Rougier in his book on Christmas Island writes of guano ruefully: "a by-product also. I found very little, although by its position and its millions of birds the island must have some"

34

But, long before that, J. D. Hague, the leading American technical authority on the guano deposits had written in 1862 of Christmas Island

"Much has been said by speculators of its rich deposits, but I have good reason to believe there is no guano worth of mention on the island. Samples that I have examined were chiefly coral sand."

And Sir Albert Ellis, the discoverer of the deposits on Nauru and Ocean Island, which have been worked ever since the turn of the century, says of Christmas succinctly: "No deposits of phosphate-guano have been located there."

This, however, is hindsight. On 20th June, 1858 Captain J. L. Pendleton of the American Guano Company ship *John Marshall* took "peaceable possession" of uninhabited Christmas Island on behalf of A. G. Benson and Associates, under a deed from Stetson. The interests changed hands twice before the end of the year and on 29th November, 1859 the United States Guano Company furnished an approved bond under the American Guano Act of 1856 by which the island was then considered "as appertaining to the United States".

This provision of the Guano Act is sometimes quoted as the basis of the American claims to Christmas Island. The Act was, however, enacted with the object of providing American agriculture with guano at lower prices than those demanded by the Peruvians, who had hitherto had a monopoly of the trade. Senator William H. Seward, of New York, introducing the bill stated "the bill itself then provides that whenever the guano should be exhausted, or cease to be found on the islands, they should revert and relapse out of the jurisdiction of the United States", which provision was upheld by the Federal Court in July 1888 in relation to the island of Navassa, similarly bonded.

The occupation was in any event short-lived, and a Danish and a British ship, wrecked on Christmas Island in 1863 and 1864 respectively, both found the island unoccupied.

British prospectors next showed an interest and a Dr. Crowther of Tasmania was granted a licence by the British Government in 1865, but when *H.M.S. Reindeer* visited on 11th June,

1868 she found "no person on the island and no appearance of any guano having been worked by anyone".

In 1869 the licence was cancelled at Dr. Crowther's own request and in 1871 a fresh licence of nine years was granted to Mr. Alfred Houlder of the London firm of Houlder Brothers & Company. When, however, Houlder's representative arrived in the Island on 5th July, 1872, he found it occupied by three employees of a Mr. C. A. Williams of the United States. He also found a board erected on the shore announcing that the U.S.S. *Narragansett* had taken possession a few days previously. Commander Meade of the *Narragansett* had been busy elsewhere that same year and amongst other acquisitions had concluded a treaty with the Chief of Tutila providing for the cession of Pago-Pago Bay in Samoa. But he was ahead of his times, for United States policy was then opposed to the extension of American sovereignty overseas and the treaty was not ratified.

Britain too was disinclined to yield to agitation by Australian and New Zealand settlers for the acquisition of outlying archipelagos of the Pacific, and it was not until Germany entered the Pacific colonial field that Britain began a process of occupation in 1884. When therefore Houlder, learning that Mr. Williams had withdrawn from Christmas Island, submitted a fresh application in 1878, the British Government was more circumspect. In January, 1879 the British Legation in Washington inquired of the Department of State whether, in view of the fact that the American firm earlier engaged in exploiting the guano on Christmas Island was reported to have given up occupation of the island, the United States had finally withdrawn its claim to the Island?

The Department of State informed the Legation that, no notice of abandonment of the Island having been received from the United States Guano Company, that company was "still considered to be entitled to the protection guaranteed by the laws of the United States in their possessory right, as far as such occupation may be necessary to secure the company or its assigns the deposits of guano found thereon".

36

So Britain did not give Mr. Houlder his permit, although *H.M.S. Pelican* on 26th September, 1880 and *H.M.S. Gannet* on 22-23rd October, 1881, both found the Island uninhabited.

Although in its exchange with the British Legation it avoided the sovereignty issue, the State Department in 1881 wrote to a Mr. A. P. Brown with reference to Christmas Island and stated that the "United States possesses no sovereign or territorial rights over that island". This was not to say, however, that America recognised the sovereignty of other nations. In 1886 for example, Secretary of State Bayard, writing to the American Minister in Chile, remarked:

"It is not easy to see how either Great Britain or Germany can assert a right to control and to divide between them insular possessions which have hitherto been free to the trade of all flags . . . If colonial acquisition were an announced policy of the United States, it is clear that this country would have an equal right to assert a claim of possession in respect of islands settled by American citizens either alone or on a footing of equality with British and German settlers."

The next step was significant in the history of Christmas Island, because on 17th April, 1882, the Master of the ship *Ryno*, belonging to Messrs Henderson and Macfarlane of Auckland, landed, hoisted the British Flag and took possession of it in the name of that firm. He left one member of his crew ashore and, apart from a gap of several years at the beginning of this century, the Island has been occupied more or less continuously ever since.

No licence was issued at that time, but the British Government was aware of the occupancy, information having been laid with the British Consulate in Samoa. This was confirmed by the visits of *H.M.S. Constance* in October, 1884, and *H.M.S. Satellite* in October, 1885, which both reported that the company had a resident Manager, Mr. Edward Freeman, living on the island with his wife and about ten workers from Penrhyn Island — Tongareva. In November, 1886 it was reported that in the four years of occupation the lagoon had produced about 200

37

tons of pearl shell, and some 18,000 to 20,000 coconuts had been planted.

Although the cable relay station was not established on Fanning Island until 1904—it continued to function there for sixty years—the project of the submarine cable from Vancouver to Queensland via Suva and Norfolk Island had been a long time in the planning. On 2nd February, 1888 the British Colonial Office took the first positive step and asked the Admiralty to send a warship to take possession of several islands, including Christmas Island, which might be needed for the cable.

On 15th March, 1888, Captain Sir William Wiseman in H.M.S. Caroline landed on Fanning Island and took possession on behalf of Her Majesty Queen Victoria. Two days later he was at Christmas Island on the same duty and found the Manager at this time was Mr. Thomas Williams, who had now only four labourers working for him. Captain Wiseman was, however, careful to report his enquiries regarding the absence of American citizens and that "observing no evidence of the island being claimed by the United States, I hoisted the flag with the same ceremonies as at Fanning Island". He continued south to annex Penrhyn and the following year Commander Nicholson of H.M.S. Cormorant followed suit for Washington Island on 29th May.

Apprised of this action by the American Minister in Honolulu, the Department of State directed the American Minister in London to recall to the attention of the British Government the correspondence exchanged in 1879. The British reply stated that the American company appeared to have abandoned the island at least as early as April 1882 and that since that time representatives of the New Zealand firm had been found in occupation. There was no evidence of any other occupation. The Commander of H.M.S. Caroline on 17th March, 1888, "had satisfied himself that there was no evidence on the spot of the island still being claimed by the United States or that it was occupied by American citizens".

The State Department took no further action in regard to

Christmas Island following this reply, nor when the island was brought within the operation of the Pacific Order in Council in 1895. Neither protest nor claim was made when, on 28th November, 1919, the boundaries of the Gilbert and Ellice Islands Colony were extended to include Christmas Island. Of necessity there have been agreements "without prejudice" — and inevitably also the occasional local *contretemps* — over the intervening years, but neither the British nor the United States Governments have sought to press the matter to a conclusion, the American attitude being that it acquiesced in the de facto British administration of the island and reserved its position. Today with the Gilbert Islands on the threshold of Independence the exchanges remain a fascinating episode in the history of the Island, but of no more than academic interest.

In 1892 Messrs Henderson & Macfarlane assigned their rights on Christmas and Suwarrow Islands to Messrs James Morrison and Co. Ltd. of London, who were granted an occupation licence for twenty-one years by the British Government for the purpose of removing guano, planting coconuts and collecting pearl shell. Henderson and Macfarlane continued to manage the island and to earn censure for their labour conditions, Commander Macvey Napier of *H.M.S. Wild Swan*, who visited the island on 5th May, 1897, reporting:

"The inhabitants are Mr. Hawk, six native men and one native woman. The natives are from Manahiki Island and are under contract to remain at Christmas at least twelve months to dive for pearl shell and collect shark fins and tails ... It seems to be custom to allow the natives at Manahiki credit to a certain amount, and then to ship them off under this twelve months contract to the various islands."

Labourers were paid an average of £3.15s.8d. per month; they were occupied primarily in diving for pearl-shell, of which they had obtained £400 worth in eight months, but, when not diving, they were expected to plant coconuts. No attempt was made to make copra, however, all spare nuts being used for planting. There were at that time 6,600 coconut trees on the

39

island and further 1,500 seed nuts from Manahiki were landed that year.

In 1898 the Island again changed hands and the Pacific Islands Company obtained a lease of ninety-nine years for this and other islands rented by the company at a joint annual rental of £200 for all the islands for five years, to be succeeded by a royalty based upon the amount of copra exported. The new Manager was a Mr. Kissling from New Zealand with a labour force of eleven from Niue Island and a progressive policy was adopted, the population growing to forty-two by December, 1902. A month or two before this report was made by *H.M.S. Shearwater*, Christmas Island had been acquired by Lever's Pacific Plantations.

In the next three years this company built two managers' houses, labourers' quarters, copra sheds and cisterns and is said to have planted 70,000 coconut trees of which, however, some seventy-five per cent died owing to a severe drought. In 1905 the company engaged an expert who planted silver lip pearl-shell, obtained from Thursday Island, in various parts of the lagoon, but a few months later the company decided to abandon their investment, said to have amounted to over £12,000 and concentrate on their more profitable holdings in the Solomon Islands. During 1906 all employees and movable property and plant were removed.

On 7th July, 1907, Commander George C. Quayle in *H.M.S. Torch* found the island deserted, as did the crew of the British steamship *Aeon*, of 5,000 tons, when she was wrecked on the south-east point on the 18th July, 1908 carrying a cargo of timber from San Francisco to Apia. The logs from the *Aeon* have lain scattered along the shore for nearly seventy years until the best were salvaged in 1976 and now make the panelling of the Bar of the newly-built "NASDA" Hotel.

In 1911 when Commander A. K. Jones of *H.M.S. Algerine* visited the island on 25th February, he found it occupied by thirteen Japanese men who had been landed a month previously by the schooner *Tobamaru*. They had already caught 11,000 birds and one of them stated that over a million had been secured by another schooner the previous year at Midway Island. The *Algerine* took the men to Fanning Island and most of them left for Tokyo in the *Tobamaru* but six were taken into employment by Father Rougier, at that time the owner of Fanning and Washington Islands, and this colourful Pacific character now enters into the history of Christmas Island.

THE ROUGIER REGIME

IF THE story of how "James, ye son of a day labourer"—as Cook was described in the baptismal record of the village church of St Cuthbert—came as Post Captain to discover Christmas Island on the other side of the world forty-nine years later is remarkable, the manner in which Petrics Emmanuel Rougier, born into a distinguished but impoverished French family in the Auvergne on 26th August, 1864, became priest, missionary, wealthy pillar of Tahiti society and sometime owner of Fanning, Washington and Christmas Islands, is bizarre.

Destined for the church, he followed normal courses of study, including two years in England and Spain, and joined the missionary Marist Fathers. On 24th June, 1888 he was ordained priest by special dispensation—he was not yet twenty-four—in order that he could go out to Fiji with a group of other young men selected by the first Roman Catholic Bishop there, Julian Vidal. He was sent directly to the delta of the Rewa River in the south-west of the main island, Vita Levu. Described by a planter who knew him at the time as "an outstanding type of man, with his long, reddish beard and forceful nature" his passion for converts and vigorous and vivacious personality was said soon to have created for him a special place. He gathered a large community together, established schools for boys and girls and built a fine church from coral limestone at Naililili.

It would be strange if such a man in nearly twenty years had not run into trouble, so it is no surprise that when he started printing old Fiji stories at his Mission press he should in those days incur the displeasure of his Bishop for propagating pagan legends. The press was closed, but he had already compiled and printed a dictionary of the Fiji language. He probably earned the Bishop's secret approbation, though awarded an official letter of reproof from the Governor of Fiji, as a result of another incident which created a furore in the correspondence columns of the *Fiji Times* of 1903. It appears that the Chief of Namosi with some 2,000 of his people were influenced by Father Rougier to forsake the Wesleyan Church for the Roman Catholic. After the baptism ceremony he collected all the old Wesleyan Bibles and replaced them with Catholic ones. Poling his punt home past the Wesleyan Mission Rougier's elation overcame his discretion and he tore up some of the Wesleyan books and scattered the leaves along the banks of the river, then at Naililili he made a glorious bonfire of the remainder to the indignation of the Wesleyan pastors.

The next year there arrived in Suva a *libéré* from the French Penal Settlement in New Caledonia, a broken middle-aged man named Cecile. No one knew the crime that sent him to the "Ile de Nou", but all reports agreed that he had been a well-educated aristocrat. Sent to the Rewa district to a French planter he soon formed a close association with Rougier and, having become a skilled artisan during his imprisonment, helped in the completion of the church. He formed an attachment with a young Fijian girl, Katarina Biaukula, and wished to marry her. Such mixed marriages were then forbidden by the Church, but after some hesitation Father Rougier performed the ceremony. He was again reproved.

This association with Cecile was the turning point in Rougier's life for about this time a letter had arrived informing Cecile that he was the heir to a large sum of money. The letter is said first to have come into Rougier's hands, and only after the marriage did he reveal its contents to Cecile. It seems Cecile put his affairs completely in the hands of Rougier, stipulating only that he and his Fijian wife should be properly provided for. Rougier went to Suva and consulted an English lawyer, Humphrey Berkeley, and within a short time the priest and lawyer were putting Cecile's fortune to good use.

Berkeley had, a year or two previously, become one of the larger partners in the plantation run by William Greig's children at Fanning and Washington. In 1907 a dispute arose between the joint owners and on a petition by Berkeley the Chief Judicial Commissioner of the Western Pacific ordered the sale of both islands by public auction in Fiji. The purchaser on 30th November, 1907 was Emmanuel Rougier for £25,000 — possibly in partnership with Berkeley. Rougier is also said to have been using part of Cecile's money for "good works", but busy tongues were at work and again the Bishop had to remonstrate. He pointed out to Rougier that as a member of a Religious Order the independent handling of money was forbidden to him. On this occasion Emmanuel Rougier stubbornly maintained that his case was an exceptional one and sought a special dispensation. The reply was said to be a proposal to transfer him to the New Hebrides. Without informing his Bishop, Father Rougier left for France, taking the young wife of Cecile with him. The exact circumstances under which he left the Mission are unclear, but although he never again practised as a priest he remained celibate and seems to have continued to regard himself as a priest in Holy Orders.

In France it appears that he mended the family fortunes and returned to the Pacific in 1910 bringing back a transformed Katarina: in the words of an old friend who met them in Vancouver—"with poise, clothes, chic and sophistication . . . a real Parisienne". She returned to her husband, but he was in ill-health and a year or two later died, probably on a visit to France.

Katarina is reported to have received no further benefit from Cecile's money and lived for some years in relative poverty. Then she married a Fijian by whom she had three children, one of whom was still alive in 1977.

Father Rougier did not return to Fiji, but about this time settled in Tahiti. He travelled in the islands, visited France and soon became a successful man of business. On 8th January, 1912 he wrote to a friend to say that he had sold Fanning and Washington Islands for the sum of £70,000 and was negotiating for the purchase of the balance of the leasehold of Christmas Island from Lever's Pacific Plantations for the sum of £10,000. He paid his first visit to Christmas from Fanning later the same year in the auxiliary schooner *Luka* of seventy tons and wrote an enthusiastic account of the island. He seems eventually to have paid £14,500 in cash and issued shares valued at £6,000 to Lever's which he presumably redeemed at some later date. His new company, Central Pacific Cocoanut Plantations Limited, registered in London, was granted an occupation licence for a term of eighty-seven years from 1st January, 1914 in return for a minimum royalty of £100 per annum.

There is some doubt about exactly when he completed the sale of Fanning and Washington Islands, because although Fanning Island Limited of London were in legal possession from about 1914, the conveyance is dated 18th March, 1918. It is also not clear whether he was still in association with Humphrey Berkeley and one report says that their association was dissolved through litigation. Certainly Rougier's resources were not augmented by his acquisition of Christmas Island and his Company accounts in 1925 showed a consolidated loss of £14,783. As a result he was granted taxation relief, a concession renewed in 1930 and again when the price of copra slumped in 1932.

For all that he was clearly a man of means and after his death in Papeete, Tahiti on 16th December, 1932 it was recorded of him in the "Pacific Islands Monthly" that:

"Père Rougier took a keen and courageous interest in all matters affecting the public welfare. He became successively President of the Chamber of Agriculture, Member of the Council of Administration, President of the Society of Oceanic Studies, of the Syndicat Agricole and of the Syndicat d'Initiative (Tourist Association) of which latter body he was the founder and continuous President since its inception ... indeed he embodied a combination of energy, ability and public spirit rarely found in any community and almost unique in the Pacific Islands. He was intensely interested in the introduction of beneficial flora and fauna and maintained an extensive garden at Taaone ... where he lived in baronial state in an old mansion surrounded by broad acres of coconut plantations ... He made considerable gifts to charity and to his church ... All his money transactions had made Father Rougier more a man of the world than a man of God. He felt it himself, and gave up all work in connexion with the Church. From that time until his death—that is, for over twenty years—he lived mostly in Papeete as a retired clergyman, saying Mass privately every day, and behaving with all the dignity of a refined gentleman."

When he was resident on Christmas Island Father Rougier at first had a cottage just to the south of the passage into the lagoon at a settlement called "Kaihau", which he later renamed "Paris" and where today only some piles of stones, a few shrubs and a lime-plastered water tank remain as witness of his occupation. Across the channel to the north was the main working settlement, as now, and he naturally called it "London"—its previous name was possibly "Tarawa". When he bought the leasehold there were about 17,000 coconut trees and between 1915 and 1936 a further 568,000 were planted, of which perhaps 400,000 survived. His other dreams for the island did not mature, but he knew it intimately and in 1924 was able to guide the "Kaimiloa" expedition to most of the archeological sites, many of which he had excavated.

He scattered the island liberally with French names and did not forget his original benefactor, who is commemorated in the "Cecile Peninsula" on the southern coast. While "St. Anne", "Bertha" and "Marthe" are to be found, "Katarina" is conspicuously absent. That a man, a priest, who earned so many good opinions should have shrugged off the wife of his friend seems to be the paradox of Rougier's life, and equally so his unsatisfactory relations with his labourers. It was indeed directly as a result of the "many complaints" . . . constantly received" as reported by the British Consul in Tahiti in 1917 that Christmas Island was brought within the boundaries of the Gilbert and Ellice Island Colony by an Order-in-Council dated 30th July, 1919 so that there could be "greater Governmental control over the conditions of employment of labourers on Christmas Island".

Specifically there had been complaints regarding the treatment of Chinese labourers, and a Tahitian, Pakoi, was put into hospital with a broken jaw and other injuries received from the American Manager, Joe Bannister English. Rougier paid full compensation to the man and his wife.

English — no relation of the John English of Fanning Island — was himself a victim of Father Rougier's inconsistencies a little later, for when the labourers were withdrawn on 29th August, 1918, having completed their time, he remained behind with a French youth and a Tahitian with a small stock of provisions and a promise that they would be picked up within forty days.

The Company's 135 ton auxiliary schooner *Ysabel May* had been beached after striking a rock off Christmas Island on 24th July. Rougier himself had directed the salvage. The ship was, however, sold to a French firm almost immediately and on 25th October, 1918 was destroyed by fire off Huahine in the Society Islands. English and his companions remained on Christmas Island without relief for nearly fourteen months until on 19th October, 1919 *H.M.S. New Zealand* happened to call. The landing party, which included Admiral of the Fleet Lord Jellicoe, was "held up" by English, in a tattered pair of shorts patched with a rice bag, brandishing a revolver. He afterwards explained that he was unaware that the War was over and thought the ship a German cruiser in disguise. An irony of their plight was that although they had no clothes, soap or other necessities and had subsisted on fish and coconuts, they had three automobiles and a good stock of fuel.

Even before this the Government of the Gilbert and Ellice Islands had refused a request from Father Rougier to be allowed to recruit his Christmas Island labour from the Gilbert Islands. No doubt they were influenced by stories brought back by those who had worked for him on Fanning and Washington.

Rakoroa Bobike, foreman for many years on Fanning Island until his death in March 1975, recalled that as a boy he had heard his elders speaking of Rougier as a "hard" master. He allowed no·waste and the child himself experienced the biscuit and rice ration, still to be eaten although rotten and weevilled.

Since 1917 an Administrative Officer had been posted to Fanning as District Commissioner of the Fanning Island District and had established his Headquarters close to the Cable Station. No official call, however, was made possible to Christmas Island until the visit of H.M.S. Calcutta on 11th March, 1922. The warship's Medical Officer made a report which was severely critical of Father Rougier's arrangements for housing, sanitation and water supplies. Similar reports were made by other visiting warships, but Rougier did not accept the criticisms and there was not much improvement.

About this time Paul Rougier, a nephew who became heir to Father Emmanuel Rougier, arrived in the Pacific and seems to have managed Christmas Island for some eleven years. He was there at the time of the visit of H.M.S. Dunedin on 25th August, 1928, together with a part-Marquesan Assistant Manager, a French foreman, eighteen Tahitian labourers, three Tahitian women, one Tubuaian woman and three children. The District Officer who travelled on the ship was critical of some of the sanitary arrangements, but stated that the labour appeared to be contented.

He must have been misled in respect of some of them, because on the night of 14/15th April, 1929 Paul Rougier awakened to find the company's launch missing and the store broken into. Missing were large quantities of provisions, several hundred gallons of fuel, a 12-bore shot gun and fifty cartridges and a compass. A surf-boat was also missing and young Rougier heard the sound of the launch outside the reef passage. Taking two labourers to row him in a dory, he attempted to close with the launch, but the three Tahitian labourers—Tefana, Nigora and Meketa—kept their distance. Paul Rougier claimed that when they threatened him with the stolen gun and made derisive signs at his suggestion that they return, he fired a shot which splintered the windscreen of the launch and then fired three more shots at the drums of gasoline and thought he had punctured two of them.

All this was reported by Father Rougier to the British Consul in Tahiti, who, referring the matter to the High Commissioner for the Western Pacific six months later, wrote:

> "Many rumours are afloat here (Tahiti) as to the causes which led up to the act. It is stated that the labourers on Christmas Island are kept in a state of indebtedness, by a system of fines for minor offences, and by exhorbitant charges for supplies from the plantation store. In this way, they are not permitted to leave the island upon the completion of their contract, thereby constituting a form of bondage . . . Also, it has been reported that the Manager, when he fired upon the boats, hit and killed two of the natives. I have been unable to establish the truthfulness of this statement; in my opinion it is extremely doubtful."

Although the High Commissioner notified the Governments of all territories in and adjoining the south Pacific, no trace of the three Tahitians was ever reported, and six years passed without a further mention of the incident. Then, early in 1936, Paul Rougier was imprisoned in Tahiti on account of "the Christmas Island affair" and telegrams flew thick and fast between the Secretary of State in London, the High Commissioner, the Resident Commissioner in Ocean Island, the British Consul-General in Tahiti, the Governor of Tahiti and the secretaries and solicitors of Rougier's company in London. The French wished to obtain permission for *une réconstitution du drame* on the spot in Christmas Island.

Paul Rougier remained in prison for four and a half months and it was then announced by the French Judicial Service that they had decided not to pursue the matter as they could not interrogate witnesses on Christmas Island, although there had been a *réconstitution* in the harbour of Papeete on 26th June. Then on 18th November, 1936 Paul Rougier was re-arrested on quite another charge—"conspiracy to defeat the ends of justice, perjury and possibly accessory before the fact in a local murder in Tahiti". He was also sentenced to two years imprisonment and a fine of five hundred francs on a charge of being in possession of a stolen confidential document.

Throughout it was the opinion of the British Consul-General that Rougier had been imprisoned for political reasons. Paul Rougier was one of a group of courageous people whose pressure for an official enquiry into the so-called "Kong-Ah" scandal in Papeete resulted in the defeat of the Government candidate as delegate to the "Conseil Superieur des Colonies".

On 24th April Paul Rougier was released on bail and left shortly afterwards for France. He was in Europe at the outbreak of war and in France lived next door to M. Henri Laval, the arch-collaborator. He became an instructor in the French Air Force, but his personal friendship for Laval led to his being sentenced to ten years forced labour by the Allied Court of Justice at Moulins on 26th October, 1945—a conviction which was quashed two years later.

Meanwhile governmental interest had moved on from cables to trans-Pacific air routes and preliminary surveys had been undertaken in the Phoenix Group and certain of the Line Islands, including Christmas Island. A party, consisting mainly of New Zealand personnel, spent some weeks on Christmas Island at the end of 1938 and the beginning of 1939 to site landing fields and a flying-boat base for Imperial Airways.

On the plantation, labour problems had continued. In 1937, following complaints by a deputation of labourers to the District Officer, the High Commissioner threatened the possible revocation of the Occupation Licence and wages were immediately raised by thirty-three per cent. In 1938 the Manager, a Czech, himself made a complaint regarding the owners when *H.M.S. Wellington* paid a visit in July. Finally on

51

30th December, 1939 all personnel in Rougier's employ were withdrawn from the Island.

A year later the secretaries and solicitors to the Company, having been unable to contact M. Paul Rougier, notified the Custodian of Enemy Property, who assumed control. The High Commissioner was authorised to work the plantation and on 4th April, 1941, *H.M.S. Monowai* arrived at Christmas Island bringing a Manager and sixteen Gilbertese and Ellice Islanders, the forerunners of a continuous occupation by the people of the Gilberts, the longest in the recorded history of the Island.

A daily weather and shipping report system was operated from then until the end of the War. At the same time a postal service was established. Previously inward and outward mail was carried by company ships and posted at the first port of call. There did exist, however, in Rougier's time a type of internal post with a local stamp which was intended to reimburse the Company for the cost and trouble of reposting. Designed by Father Rougier, it was first mentioned in the philatelic press in July 1916 and covers exist dated 1918. It continued until 1938.

The basic design of the stamps was printed in five colours and shows a schooner, presumed to be the *Ysabel May*, arriving at its anchorage off a palm-studded island, where it is being welcomed by flocks of sea-birds, while a golden-red sun is setting in a very blue ocean. The first issue was for "5 Cents", which was said to be the equivalent of 5 Cents American, 25 French centimes or $2\frac{1}{2}$d. in British money. There were four issues, on the third of which, in 1926, the denomination was raised to "10 Cents" and there were minor changes in the wording, but the basic design remained the same.

The Gilbert Islands Christmas season stamp issue this year, 1977, consists entirely of stamps commemorating Cook's discovery of the island.

MILITARY VISITATIONS

MANY CALLS by warships of the Royal Navy have been chronicled. These visits were of a peaceful nature, concerned with the watch and ward which the Navy maintained over those Pacific islands for which Britain had in one way or another assumed responsibility, or where British subjects were otherwise inclined to regard themselves as outside the law.

In the First World War the Line Islands had not entirely escaped attention. Scarcely had hostilities broken out in 1914 when the German Cruiser *Nuremberg* landed a raiding party at the Fanning Island cable station, blew up the power station, cut the trans-Pacific cable and towed the ends out to sea. From there they were, however, quickly retrieved by Hugh Greig, grandson of the former owner, in a remarkable feat of seamanship. Emergency repairs soon had communications re-established.

The German Admiral von Spee stayed off Christmas Island from 7th to 9th September and then steamed south for Cape Horn and the Falkland Islands, where shortly afterwards his Squadron was vanquished.

The surveys on Christmas Island, which had started with peaceful trans-ocean passenger services in mind in the late 1930s, were, after the outbreak of the Second World War, resumed in April, 1941 by the New Zealand Forces and a start was made on deepening the London passage into the lagoon. Later in the year the United States sent a party of twenty-seven military men and civilians, with the goodwill of the British Government, to look for a suitable site for an aerodrome, one of a chain of landing fields to be built across the Pacific for the heavy bombers on their way to the Far East.

The American wartime occupation began when the Air Transport ship *Haleakala* arrived on 18th November, 1941 with eight officers, 155 enlisted men of the U.S. Corps of Engineers and more than eighty civilians to begin the construction of the airfield. The Japanese attack on Pearl Harbour, 1,200 miles to the north, came less than a month later.

Soon after, two 155 mm. guns and two 75 mm. guns with artillerymen were sent for the protection of the Island and on 11th February, 1942 the S.S. *President Johnson* landed a task force under Colonel Paul W. Rutledge, bringing the establishment to 2,428 soldiers and 193 civilians. This was the highest total achieved during the United States occupation, which lasted until 15th October, 1948, by which time there were less than 500 men remaining. The Island was given the code name of "BIRCH".

The first concern was for the three-runway airfield near the north-eastern coast constructed by 804th Aviation Bn. with six inches of compacted lagoon mud on eight inches of compacted coral gravel. The main runway was 7,000 feet long and 200 feet wide and forms the base of the existing airfield. In August, 1942 the dredger *Monarch* arrived and was joined in January, 1943 by the *Sacramento*. Between them they removed 338,000 cubic yards from the lagoon bed as part of a plan to dredge a channel thirty feet deep and one hundred feet wide from the Cook Passage to the east of London. There a 1,000 foot square turning basin would front a wharf, giving a minimum of twenty-six feet of water alongside. The wharf—still in restricted use—was completed at a length of 370 feet with fifty-foot wing walls, but when in April, 1943 the dredgers had reached a depth of something between fifteen and twenty feet, they were sent away to some area of higher priority in the Pacific war, where the tide of Japanese advance had turned and the Battle of Tarawa was in the making.

The defence of Christmas Island, with ninety miles of coastline, presented problems for the small force and efforts were therefore concentrated on protecting the airfield from commando raids. The remains of the network of underground machine-gun nests can still be traced between the airfield and the ocean shore. In fact there were no raids or engagements in the Line Islands, but for a long time the garrison on Christmas was troubled by shortages, complaints and low morale. The civilians all wanted to be discharged after Pearl Harbour, being in fear for their families in Hawaii, and the airfield had priority over living quarters and other amenities. Two fires broke out in November, 1942 and emphasized the need for more fire-fighting equipment, and 100 tons of dynamite, valued at U.S.$ 23,000, exploded accidentally on Cook Island on 24th February, 1943.

However things were already on the mend and four miles north of London, in an area still marked as "The Farm", large-scale hydroponic cultivation of vegetables was begun and by August, 1942, 39 cattle, 130 pigs, 275 chickens, 100 ducks and several rabbits were in residence, although most of their fodder had to be imported.

Meanwhile the Gilbertese brought in to work the plantation had been diverted to help the American forces, and only at the end of 1942 was the cutting of copra resumed. Additional labour was brought in and some thirty to forty tons a month were harvested thereafter and exported to the Allied International Copra Pool in San Francisco.

Even before the departure of the American Forces, Madame Alice Calamy-Rougier, a sister of Paul Rougier, had begun to press on behalf of her brother for indemnities and for the resumption of his occupation of the island, visiting Suva for talks with the High Commission. The Government of the Gilbert and Ellice Islands, however, now saw Christmas Island as an answer to the overpopulation problem of the home islands, which had already led to a resettlement scheme in the Phoenix Group and the purchase of two islands in the Fiji Group. On 14th June, 1949 therefore the Rougier family sold the balance of their interest in the lease for £50,000 sterling, of which £14,000 represented the profits which had accrued from the working of the plantation since 1941.

The Native Lands Commissioner of the time, H. E. Maude, after his first visit in 1938, had estimated that Christmas Island could absorb 8,000 settlers. In 1946 he revised this downwards to 6,500, but the following year he recognised the great variability of the rainfall and suggested only a small experimental settlement, the major migration targets to be Fanning and Washington. On 25th January, 1946 the Fanning Islands District was renamed the Line Islands District and in 1965 the Headquarters moved to Christmas Island.

In pursuance of the new settlement policy a group of thirty-six landless men from the island of Aranuka in the Gilberts were brought to Christmas Island in September 1949 on a contract basis and a year later their families joined them. They had the ill-fortune in 1950 to experience one of the two years of lowest rainfall ever recorded, only seven inches. They declared it was impossible to grow breadfruit or "babai"—a root crop of the Taro family—which are staples of the Gilbertese diet, and demanded repatriation. In consequence, in March, 1951 they returned home and no further attempts have been made to bring in settlers. On the contrary the policy was to continue to run the plantation through the wholly government-owned Christmas Island Plantation company and to bring in labour on three year contracts for married men and two years for single. Recruiting ships were shared with Fanning Island Plantations, but due to the expense of the operation the practice was slowly replaced by the employment of a semi-permanent labour force on Fanning and Washington, and Christmas Island followed suit.

Copra production fluctuated with the uncertain rainfall, reaching a peak of 867 tons in 1950 and generally averaging about 600 tons, but other factors were soon to bring copra cutting to a standstill again.

Towards the end of 1953 there was a small flutter in the political dovecotes of the Pacific when word reached the High Commission that the United States intended to set up a Government Fishery and Wild Life Field Establishment on Christmas Island. Police reinforcements were hurriedly dispatched. Before they could arrive, however, the Secretary of State for the Colonies had instructed that he wished every reasonable assistance and facility to be given to the Fish and Wild Life Service Mission. Concealing their tin helmets and firearms as they landed, therefore, the party devoted their energies to helping the four-man scientific expedition in their search for tuna bait, poison fish and the setting up of water thermographs and other weather recording instruments. All was peace and goodwill, and, after their departure two months later, the maintenance and reading of the Mission equipment was left to the care of the Island's mechanic and radio operator.

Another visitor on the same ship was a Captain E. E. Johnson of the Robert Dollar Company of San Francisco. He wished to make a survey of the Island's facilities for use as a refuelling stop for South Pacific Air Line operating "Solent" flying boats to Tahiti. His mission was, however, doomed to be dogged by misfortune.

His principals unwittingly had made a tactical political error in obtaining from the Secretary to the United States Air Force a lease for twenty years of Casady Airfield and the sea-plane base —which had been established south of Paris—together with the use of the Christmas Island roads and dock. As a result the British Representatives in the Pacific, who had not been consulted, engaged the Company and its officials in twelve months of frustration. Even four months after the British Government had notified the American State Department that it "looks forward with anticipation to the institution of operations by South Pacific Airlines to Christmas Island in the near future, and has no desire to interfere with or obstruct the establishment of such an operation", the District Officer was being told to "play for time without appearing un-cooperative".

The Engineer-in-Charge, R. S. Mills, protested that "there is apparently no feeling that the air service will be of any benefit to the Island" and proposed that the airline overfly. But, perhaps unfortunately at this late hour, the difficulties dissolved and on 4th March, 1956 a 175-foot barge of 592 tons, drawing five feet of water, docked at London with supplies for building the base. A small hotel with four bedrooms, a lounge, refrigeration, laundry equipment and outbuildings was erected together with a 141-foot radio beacon and two 25 kw generators. Trucks, tractor, crane, low-loader, tanks, tanker-trailers and a launch were all in readiness for the first flight to take place not later than June.

Then suddenly on 21st April the Hawaiian newspapers and radio reported that Christmas Island was to be the base for staging the British H-Bomb tests. Mills sent a frantic telegram and was assured that the air operation of S.P.A.L. would not be affected. Fourteen days later he was instructed to prepare to abandon the project. The British Ministry of Defence paid compensation in full, the hotel was left as it stood and still exists as a relic of that episode. Ten years later a Stratocruiser landed at Christmas Island on a proving flight for emergency landings, the only plane of S.P.A.L. ever to visit the Island.

The first step in the selection of Christmas Island as the Bomb Test Base had in fact been taken in January and February of 1956, when *H.M.N.Z.S. Lachlan* brought a survey party to the Island to "bring information up to date in connection with the International Geo-Physical Year". In March a request was received for the clearing of the runways at the airport and early in April information was received that the British Government was to establish an "Air Base" at Christmas Island and the code name "GRAPPLE" was born.

The official announcement that the real purpose was the testing of nuclear weapons followed and on 19th June, 1956 the advance party for the operation arrived. By July a canvas town had appeared and there were two thousand sailors, soldiers and airmen on the Island, apart from the crews of the vessels in port and the civilian scientific personnel. Recording stations were established on Malden and Fanning Islands. At first there were suggestions from the Gilbert and Ellice Islands Government that the island should be evacuated, but this was said to be unnecessary and in fact additional workers were sent for employment by the Forces. However, in February 1957 all the women and children and most of the plantation staff were evacuated to Fanning Island where they remained until 22nd June.

Three bombs in the megaton range were successfully dropped by "Valiant" bombers and exploded at about 18,000 feet some thirty miles south of the island between 15th May and 19th June. The thirty-three government staff and plantation workers, who had remained on the Island, were taken aboard a Naval Landing Craft for the explosions, which took place very early in the morning while they watched a film show below decks. Instructions provided for all doors and windows to be left open and all breakables to be placed flat on the floor. Very little damage was reported—except by those who neglected these instructions. Evacuation of the military personnel, apart from a caretaker force, began in July, but meanwhile a decision had been taken in England to develop the Island as a 5-Years Trials Base. Some materials already loaded in the port were unloaded and in August a build-up began which, over the next two years, was to produce a reconstruction of the wharf and port, the resurfacing and sealing of the main runway of the American-built airfield with the installation of hangars, control tower and many other facilities. Another 6,000-foot sealed runway was constructed at the extreme end of the south-east arm—"Aeon Field" taking its name from the former wreck. An asphalt road twenty miles long was built from London to the airfield, extending a further thirty-five miles of single-width to the south-east point. Hutted camps with power-station, piped water and sanitation and recreational facilities were built three miles west of the airfield—"Main Camp"—

and at London—"Port Camp"—to house a total of about four thousand men at the peak of the constructional and operational programmes.

In November of 1957 there were two further H-Bomb explosions and between April and September of 1958 a further series. There was no evacuation to Fanning Island for these tests, but all were taken to off-shore boats—except at the time of some low-power bomb detonations, when even that was not considered necessary. With the prevailing easterly winds the dangers from radio-activity was said to be nil and very minimal for "blast". Only the danger to eyes from "flash" made it essential for people to be under cover.

In April, 1959 H.R.H. the Duke of Edinburgh visited the Base during a Pacific tour. With talks on the banning of further bomb explosions in the atmosphere beginning in Geneva, activity was minimal. Towards the end of the year it was announced that personnel would be reduced to 1700 by 1st January, 1960 and to 300 in July. Christmas Island was now being envisaged as a transit base for the Far East and R.A.F. Transport Command took over. Copra cutting resumed in November, 1959.

But it was not after all to be quite the end of military activity. The Geneva talks broke down and American Defence Chiefs were pressing for a resumption of tests. President Kennedy finally approved and Britain accepted that they should be staged at Christmas Island, which now was given yet another code name—"DOMINIC". On 15th February, 1962 fifty men from the American firm of Holmes and Narver arrived to reactivate the Main Camp and within two weeks there were more than 800 American servicemen and civilians on the island. Numbers rose rapidly, until by the time of the first "shot" on 25th April there were 3,500 British and American personnel engaged. Between then and 11th July there was a total of twenty-four "shots" in the series. Other tests were going on at Johnston Island 1,200 miles to the north-west and on 8th July it was recorded that the midnight high-altitude explosion there was clearly visible on Christmas Island.

Evacuation to off-shore ships was not considered necessary, but after two heavy explosions people became nervous and voluntary arrangements were made. Almost total for the next test, evacuation soon fell below half and only about a third of the people, including all the children, were leaving the island by the end of the series. Those still on shore went to the *maneabas* and waited with bowed heads and closed eyes for the countdown, for "flash" was still the danger. They were then free to go outside and see for the first time the boiling flames of the "mushroom" cloud and experience the delayed shock waves and the roar of the explosion.

At the beginning of 1963 there was talk of the establishment of a permanent American satellite tracking station on Christmas Island, but interest waned and by the end of September the last of the American servicemen had departed. In Britain, too, strategic imperatives were changing and the Christmas Island base was an early casualty of the withdrawal of British Forces from the Pacific theatre. In June the last inventories were made, obsolete and dangerous materials were dumped at sea, the offices were locked and at sunset on Monday 29th June, 1964 the White Ensign was lowered at the Royal Navy shore station, *H.M.S. Resolution*.

American service personnel reappeared very briefly in April, 1970 to stand by on Christmas Island for the "splash-down", two hundred miles to the south, of the Apollo 13 crew returning from the moon.

After the departure of the Forces, Operation "Hard Look" had carried out a full investigation into the possibilities of radioactive contamination, but had found none. In 1975 a further examination of Christmas Island was undertaken by American experts as part of the preparation for the establishment of a Japanese tracking station. They reported that radio-activity levels were lower than those found in most American cities and that there was nothing on the island which could lead an investigator to deduce that there had ever been an atomic detonation in the vicinity.

NEW PERSPECTIVES

FOR FIVE years after 1964 the future of the military installations remained in the balance. Then abandonment was finally decided upon and Christmas Island was steadily stripped of all those moveable items for which a use could be visualised. Thus Tarawa, capital of the Gilbert Islands since the war, received its first telephone system from the Main Camp, electrical generators, tar sealing for some of its roads, vehicles, plant, beds, carpets, crockery, shirts and shorts, cable and building materials, while military warehouses now silhouette the skyline of Gilbert and Ellice Islands.

On Christmas itself the villages of London and Poland were reconstructed from military hutments and a new village was built near the airport, taking the Army name of "Banana" from the waterhole there, and replacing the old villages situated at the nearby American camp and at Four Wells. Plant and vehicles were taken into use and kept running by a constant process of cannibalisation. Some are still in use today, as are the electricity and water systems established by the Royal Engineers.

Everywhere the salt-laden winds have taken their toll and there are few corners of the island which are not marked by the detritus of military occupation: bulldozers abandoned where they last broke down, black patches where bitumen has oozed from a dump of rusted drums, a small mountain of beer cans and bottles outside the skeleton of a one-time canteen, porcelain urinals standing like monuments upon the foundations of a former toilet block and everywhere trailing wires, the lurching frames of former offices, messrooms and workshops, while packing cases spill their contents of mysterious spares for installations long-since obsolete.

In 1966 the Government commissioned a full-scale land resource study of the coconut growing potential of Christmas Island and this was undertaken by Messrs R. N. Jenkin and M. A. Foale on behalf of the British Directorate of Overseas Surveys. They found that although much of the land already planted was relatively unproductive, there were 10,887 acres of unused land suitable for planting, of which some 5,000 acres were most promising with very favourable groundwater conditions. They predicted that full development and improved cultivation methods could produce a yield of more than 2,500 tons of copra a year.

The government plantation company had in 1961 resumed a modest programme of planting, but the full proposed expansion has yet to be implemented. Today there are some 13,500 acres under cultivation and annual production is in the region of 600 tons of dried copra. After the war the company had the benefit of a long-term contract with a guaranteed price from the British Ministry of Food, but since then has been at the mercy of the very erratic copra market. Two ships of the Bank Line call each year to bring in supplies and load the copra from Christmas, Fanning and Washington Islands. Ships of the Gilbert's Government fleet also call about once every three or four months to maintain communications with the home islands.

In this manner Christmas Island continued the even tenor of its way until in 1971 Dr. P. Helfrich of the Hawaiian Institute of

Top: *an aerial view of Cook Island.*

Left: *Hermit Crabs at South East Point.*

Stamps to commemorate the bicentenary of Captain Cook's discovery of Christmas Island.

ix

X

Above: *Christmas (Casady) Airport.*

Left: *the Civil Engineer's residence at London.*

Below: *Downrange Station No3, NASDA tracking station.*

Right: *dancers in traditional costume.*

Above & left:
Catholic mission
meniaba, *London*.

Above: *a palm of the "Niningaum" (thousand nuts) type.*

Above centre: *preparing explosive charges.*

Right: *the finished product —a brine shrimp channel.*

Above: *corner stone of the chapel at an abandoned British Forces site on the North Shore. The inscription reads "This stone was laid on 12th Sept. 1958 by Revd. E. G. Alsop, RAF, on the completion of this church".*

Top: *a young red-footed booby.*

Above: *adult blue-faced boobies.*

Right: *brine shrimp project. Feeding milkfish to the frigate birds.*

xvi

Marine Biology led a team to investigate the potential of the island for the production of the Brine Shrimp—*Artemia salina*. This tiny marine animal is in constant demand by aquaria and fish farmers for the vital part which it can play as a food source for newly hatched fish. A can of eggs was left behind for scattering on the salt ponds and three years later, when the Gilbert Islands Development Authority decided to sponsor commercial production, *artemia* was found to be flourishing. Today the scheme is moving steadily towards the first full-scale attempt at intensive culture in the world.

The brine shrimp—pinkish, almost transparent, half-an-inch in length with two pin-point black eyes—is a desert animal which has the habit of producing live young in favourable conditions and egg-like cysts when declining food supplies and rising salinity give warning that the pool is likely to dry. These cysts resemble fine grey dust and have a tough outer covering which can withstand buffeting about the countryside in heat and cold for several years. But within forty-eight hours of re-immersion in fresh water the shrimp will emerge to reach sexual maturity in about two weeks and recommence the life-cycle, producing up to 200 young every five days.

To simulate this natural life cycle a number of the island's 200 lagoons have been linked by channels to achieve a controlled tidal flow. Salinity levels can thus be manipulated, while cyclical fertilization of the ponds is aimed to boost the food supply and the brine shrimp population to optimum levels. When the supply of nutrients is cut off the animals react to the stressed conditions. They begin to lay eggs which are harvested to form a valuable export and support to the economy of the Gilbert Islands.

To make this rhythmic intensive culture possible it was necessary to clear the ponds of fish and it was found that milk-fish—Chanos chanos—which are known to tolerate fresh water, could also survive in salinity levels of up to 140 parts per thousand—about three times as salt as ocean water. Even more remarkable was the confirmation of milk-fish breeding in the ponds, the first time this has ever been observed anywhere in the world: although in this the scientists were several years behind the Gilbertese fishermen.

With the imminent exhaustion of the phosphate deposits on Ocean Island—Banaba—and the consequent loss of the main source of the country's foreign exchange, the Gilbertese Government has turned its attention more closely to the potential of Christmas Island. In 1975 a team from the Royal Engineers carried out an examination of the residue of the military installations and reported their usefulness as a support for the island infrastructure. Another survey of the economic possibilities of Christmas, together with Fanning and Washington was undertaken in 1977 as was a specialist appraisal of the progress and prospects of the Brine-shrimp Project.

In 1975 the National Space Development Agency of Japan was invited to select Christmas Island as a down-range station for their programme of satellite launching. Supported by the American T.R.W. Corporation, a tracking site was set up in the Four Wells area in 1976 and played an important role in the successful launch on 22nd February, 1977 and the orbit location a few days later.

To serve the engineers manning the station a 48-bed hotel was constructed and a weekly air charter, flown by a Pacific American DC6, operated for a period of twelve months between Christmas Island and Honolulu, with half the flights continuing to Tarawa. Today the Gilbert Islands Government's own internal air service Air Tungaru operates a service with a Boeing "727", chartered from Air Nauru. This operates weekly between Tarawa in the Gilberts and Honolulu via Christmas Island.

Although tourist development is encouraged to help to make the air service an economic proposition, it is important that it remains at modest levels. Huge seabird colonies, which are the outstanding attraction and are famous in scientific circles, have to be guarded against excessive disturbance. Christmas Island has been the centre of important seabird studies, notably that of the Pacific Ocean Biological Survey Program (P.O.B.S.P.) of the Smithsonian Institution.

66

Two hundred years ago Captain James Cook, writing of the fauna of the Island had this to say:

Under the low trees above-mentioned, fat infinite num-bers of a new fpecies of tern, or egg-bird. Thefe are black above, and white below, with a white arch on the fore-head; and are rather larger than the common noddy. Moft of them had lately hatched their young; which lay under old ones, upon the bare ground. The reft had eggs; of which they only lay one, larger than that of a pigeon, bluifh and fpeckled with black. There were alfo a good many common boobies; a fort that are almoft like a gan-net; and a footy, or chocolate-coloured one, with a white belly. To this lift we muft add men-of-war-birds; tropic-birds; curlews; fand-pipers; a fmall land-bird like a hedge-fparrow; land-crabs; fmall lizards; and rats.

There are in fact eighteen species of sea-bird which regularly nest on Christmas Island. The sooty-tern, which was new to Cook, is found in colonies numbering millions and has the habit, unobserved elsewhere, of having two breeding seasons each year, in June and December. Not only are other species numerous, but because Christmas Island is a Wild Life Sanctuary, they are not afraid of humans and can be approached and observed at close quarters without difficulty. It is possible on Christmas Island to walk under a cloud of wheeling birds reminiscent of Hitchcock's film version of "The Birds", to watch the antics of the fluffy Disney-like chicks of the blue-faced booby and sometimes, at night, to hear the strange human moaning of the shearwaters flying in to their colonies.

In recognition of this resource the World Wildlife Fund is supporting a Gilbert's Government scheme of research, protec-tion and conservation and the British Government has appointed Mr. Roger Perry, formerly Director of the Charles Darwin Institute in the Galapagos Islands, to carry it through. Although generally the natural populations both avian and marine, appear to have been stable since the days of Cook, their vulnerability can be gauged by experiences elsewhere in the Pacific where large breeding populations have entirely disappeared.

Reference has already been made to the very small numbers of green turtle where they were once abundant; the former large colonies of red-tailed tropic bird, whose long-feathers are prized and which themselves are said to be good eating, have been much reduced in recent years; the taking of tern eggs for food has had to be prohibited as the human population has grown to nearly one thousand. At the same time feral cats have become formidable predators and one observer counted as many as seventy-five sooty-tern carcases daily in one colony alone.

Perhaps the largest single destructive force was the H–Bomb era. The survey found very low radio-activity levels, but the birds could not be protected from "flash". Millions were blinded and in consequence died from starvation and, although there has been a remarkable recovery in the ensuing fifteen years, some colonies were virtually exterminated. The construction of roads and airfields, with increasing levels of ground and air traffic, the disturbance to the ecology by developmental activities, all have their effect in varying degrees, the long-range consequences of which cannot be foreseen. To monitor these changes and to guard a precious natural heritage is a matter of concern to the Gilbert's Government which is expressed in its recent Wildlife Conservation Ordinance and the setting up of the conservation unit on Christmas Island. This, it is hoped, will be able to extend its surveillance to other islands of the group.

And the workers of Christmas Island, almost by accident, have become a community. The land is entirely owned by the Government and all the people therefore retain strong family links with their home islands, where they have their "lands", still the core of Gilbertese stability.

But key staff have been encouraged to extend their contracts, so that today many have nearly thirty years service on the island. In this time their children have grown up and married and have their families at school. Many have spent their entire lives on the island and have never seen their "homes".

The small group which arrived thirty-six years ago was augmented by a further fifty-one from the Gilberts in 1943 and forty from the Ellice Islands in 1945. Ten years later there was a population of seventy-four workers, twenty-nine wives and fifty-one children of whom twenty-two were attending the first school. During the Bomb Test period numbers were increased, but in September 1964, 189 men, women and children were repatriated to their home islands. Those left behind showed an increase at 278, and the census of 1968 numbered them at 367 and that of 1973 at 674. Recruitment for the development work now in progress on the island has raised the labour force to over 300 with another thirty in government service. The total is in the vicinity of 1000 and there are 120 children in the three village schools, which offer a full primary course.

Since the first occupation there has been a daily radio schedule to Tarawa and since 1965 there has been a government Medical Officer in residence and a small hospital. Today the government services, headed by an Administrative Officer, now separated from the management of the Plantation Company, include an Inspector of Police in charge of the Line Islands and eight other ranks, customs, postal, meteorological and aircraft control officers and the teachers. A labour union, which covers most employed workers in the country, maintains a small office. Both the Gilbert Islands Protestant Church and the Roman Catholic Mission are strongly established in all three centres of population, and much of the social activity of the island, as elsewhere in the Gilbert Islands, revolves around the churches.

Although the reconstruction of the villages swept away the traditional thatched houses and all able-bodied men and many women are in employment, the social structure of Gilbertese life remains. The very small number of pandanus trees—the screw pine—inhibits the exercise of skills like mat, hat and basket weaving, but the ancient forms of Gilbertese dance and song, choir singing and other activities and pastimes—in all of which the emphasis is on participation—continue regularly. These take place mainly in the *maneabas*, the large open-sided meeting houses which are, on all islands, at the heart of community life. Store goods, of which rice, flour, hard biscuits — derived from the old sailing ships' "bread", sugar, tobacco, matches, soap and kerosene are the staples, have not displaced the basic diet of fish and the many products of the coconut palm — the Pacific "tree of life".

Fishing by line, net and spear, the people of Christmas Island have little difficulty in keeping their families well supplied. Although the inshore catches are less prolific than in earlier years, few canoes are seen, for there is little necessity yet to exploit the further waters of the lagoon. A few modern boats powered by outboard engines fish the off-shore waters of the ocean reef for tuna, jack and king-fish; while on dark nights at low tide wavering lights show where the lobsters and octopus are being harvested on the reef itself.

Some of the finest tuna grounds in the Pacific are in the vicinity of the Line Islands and Korean and Taiwanese long-liners are frequently seen and not infrequently end their days on the island reefs — most recently one on Christmas Island in 1976 and two wrecked at Malden in 1977. The Island is also a rendezvous for yachts crossing the Pacific by way of Honolulu, the Marquesas, Tahiti or Samoa. Some drawing less than six feet enter the lagoon, but the entrance to the wharf is too silted for deeper craft and they lie off the reef, the prevailing easterly wind keeping them safe from the rocks.

Among the future plans under consideration is one to replace the present system of working larger vessels by lighter through the construction of a deep-water jetty in the western ocean bay north of London. Here today the iron ships ride safely at anchor on "a bank of fine sand" as did those redoubtable wooden vessels the *Resolution* and the *Discovery* just two hundred years ago when Christmas Island's recorded history began, penned at a "good anchorage, in any depth between eighteen and thirty fathoms" by Captain James Cook.

APPENDICES

FACTS ABOUT
CHRISTMAS ISLAND
72
BIRDS OF
CHRISTMAS ISLAND
76

Facts about Christmas Island

Location: The largest coral atoll in the world with an area of 248 square miles of which 125 square miles is land and the remainder lagoons. Lies between longitudes 157° 10' w and 157° 34' w and latitudes 1° 42' N, and 2° 03' N, 145 miles north of the Equator.

Mean Height: Above sea level five to twelve feet: highest point "Joe's Hill"—forty-three feet.

Distances: Tarawa 2015 miles, Fanning Island 175 miles, Washington Island 265 miles, Apia 1500 miles, Tahiti 1450 miles, Honolulu 1335 miles, Suva 2150 miles, Sydney 4000 miles, San Francisco 3250 miles.

Climate: Equatorial Dry Zone with average annual rainfall of 873 mm (thirty-four ins), but varying from very dry 177 mm (seven ins—1954) to wet 2621 mm (103 ins—1941); a diurnal temperature fluctuating between 30°C (86°F) and 24°C (76°F), an average relative humidity of seventy per cent relieved by a more or less constant easterly wind of an average of eight knots and an average cloud cover of four-eighths.

Population (1977): Mainly Micronesian from the Gilberts archipelago, .with a small group of Polynesians from Tuvalu (Ellice Islands) and ten expatriates: total 1091—adults 648 and children 443.

Government: Since 1952 Headquarters of the Line Islands District of the self-governing colony of the Gilbert Islands. Under British administration since 1888, Independence is planned for 1978. An Administrative and Licensing Office, Divisional Police Office and Post Office operate in regular office hours from 8.00 am to 12.30 pm and 1.30 pm to 4.15 pm Monday to Friday. Christmas Island is a Closed District and all persons require a licence to stay on the island.

Customs: Christmas Island is the Port of Entry for the Line Islands for Customs and Quarantine.

Immigration: All visitors require a valid passport: a visa, obtainable from British consulates, is required by all visitors except holders of British and Commonwealth passports and those of Belgium, Denmark, Finland, Greece, Iceland, Italy, Netherlands, Norway, Sweden, Spain, Switzerland, Turkey, Tunisia and Uruguay. Persons without visas may be allowed to land on payment of a fee of A$5.00 or US$6.00. Application for a permit to enter and reside must be made to the Principal Immigration Officer, Tarawa, well in advance for any stay exceeding sixty days. A valid vaccination certificate for small-pox is normally required and for cholera and yellow fever by persons travelling from countries where these diseases are endemic.

Medical: A Medical Officer is in residence with a small hospital. Serious emergencies can be evacuated to Honolulu by U.S. Coastguard "Hercules". There is no malaria. Dental treatment is confined to extractions.

Communications:
Air: Christmas (Casady) Airfield has a tarmac runway of 6,900 feet and can take the largest planes flying. A non-directional beacon is available on request and a Flight Service Officer and Fire Service attend the airport. Meteorological reports are available.
Sea: Gilbert's ships visit the Line Islands three or four times each year and a Bank Line vessel calls twice a year to land cargo and uplift the copra crop. There are intermittent visits by fuel tankers and tourist ships. Small craft drawing less than six feet of water can reach the wharf east of London via the London or Cook Passages and there are good anchorages off the ocean reef

73

to the west of London. The tidal range is between fifty-one inches at springs and sixteen inches at neaps.

Telegraphic: schedules for internal and overseas telegrams via Tarawa operate three times daily; emergency messages can be relayed during week-days through a private telex link to the University of Hawaii; there is no telephone service or voice link. Principal offices and vehicles are linked by C.B. Radio.

Mails: are dispatched through Tarawa or Honolulu as opportunity offers and the addresses for inward mail are either "via Tarawa, the Gilbert Islands" or "The Gilbert Islands, via P.O. Honolulu, Hawaii, U.S.A.".

Vehicles: can be hired when available: Station Wagons (tarmacadam roads only—fifty-five miles London to S.E. Point) A$18 per day plus fuel or forty cents per mile (1977); Land Cruisers A$23 per day plus fuel or forty-five cents per mile; Pick-Ups A$18 per day plus fuel or thirty-five cents per mile. There were in August 1977 thirty licensed cars and 151 licensed motor cycles on the island in addition to thirty-six trucks and mobile plant, including a 20-ton crane on the wharf. Foreign driving licenses are recognised as valid for fourteen days.

Economy: The currency is the Australian Dollar. There is no Bank, but Travellers Cheques in international currencies and cash in Sterling or U.S. Dollars can be exchanged at the Government Office. There is an internal Telegraph Money Order system and money from overseas can be transmitted through the Bank of New South Wales in Tarawa.

All the Island is Crown Land and 12,767 acres are planted with coconuts under the management of Atoll Plantations Limited, a wholly Gilbert's Government owned company producing an average of 570 tons of copra per annum. An intensive cultivation system for the production of brine shrimp *(see text)* is under development in the lagoon area. The National Space Development Agency of Japan operates a satellite tracking station on the island: next shot February, 1979. The

NASDA Hotel is a Government-owned and operated forty-eight-bed hotel two miles from the airport, fully air-conditioned: flat rate—A$25.00 per day with full board (1977). There are thirty government employees and approximately 300 other persons in employment on the island in the above enterprises and their servicing, with an aggregate income of A$30,000 per month. Trade stores in the three centres of population sell basic items of foodstuffs and other necessities. Fresh food is not generally available on the island other than fish and coconuts, the staples of the Gilbertese diet.

Services: Good ground water is pumped to all inhabited areas. Sanitation is by septic tank. Electricity is generated at 240 v. 50 cy. at London, Banana and Poland and is available for two hours in the morning and three hours in the evening and otherwise as required. A twenty-four-hour supply at 110 v. 60 cy. is provided at the tracking station, hotel and brine shrimp installation.

Education: Primary schools offering eight years of education are established at the three villages and are attended by 260 pupils aged six to fifteen years (1977). Secondary and Technical education is provided in the Gilbert Islands, at Tarawa, Beru and Abaiang.

Justice: is administered on the island by an Island Court drawn from a panel of Local Members. There is a Magistrate on the Island, but offences with a liability for sentences exceeding one year's imprisonment are tried by a visiting Senior Magistrate or the High Court sitting in Tarawa.

Birds of Christmas Island

Christmas Island has seabird colonies of worldwide scientific importance with eighteen species nesting regularly on the main island and lagoon islets. The one land bird that nests is the Christmas Island warbler. The majority of species are protected by law, and three areas—Cook Island, Motu Upua and Motu Tabu—have been designated bird sanctuaries with restricted access. A Wildlife Conservation Unit, with a resident warden at London, will assist visitors interested in seeing bird colonies. Visitors are reminded of the great care needed at all times in seabird nesting areas, not only to avoid trampling eggs and young but to prevent damage to sheltering scrub and to prevent injury underfoot to burrow-nesting petrels and shearwaters.

Species List: Gilbertese names appear in brackets.
WEDGE-TAILED SHEARWATER (Korobaro) *Puffinus pacificus* Nests in shallow burrows on main island and lagoon islets from May onwards. Largely nocturnal in colonies. Few birds present during December and January.
CHRISTMAS SHEARWATER (Tinebu) *Puffinus nativitatis* Nests in shallow tunnels or scrapes under bushes on lagoon islets. Resident; individuals found nesting throughout year.
AUDUBON'S SHEARWATER *Puffinus lherminieri* Least common breeding seabird. Nests recorded on islets in Isles Lagoon.
DUSKY or LITTLE SHEARWATER (Nna) *Puffinus assimilis* Sight records in 1958. Straggler from temperate Southern Pacific.
PHOENIX PETREL (Tangiuoua or Ruru) *Pterodroma alba* Common resident species. Nests in burrows on un-disturbed lagoon islets.
WHITE-THROATED STORM PETREL (Bwebwe-ni-marawa) *Neso-fregetta albigularis* Small population of several hundreds, nesting in hollows, burrows or crevices in coral on lagoon islets.
RED-TAILED TROPICBIRD (Taake) *Phaeton rubricauda* Common throughout year, especially during peak nesting period June to October. Nests on main island and islets, on ground, in full shade. Formerly persecuted for its long tail streamers.

RED-FOOTED BOOBY (Kota or Makitaba) *Sula sula* Common resident, breeding throughout much of year, primarily in central lagoon area. A favourite nesting tree is the Ren (*Messerschmidia argentea*). Juveniles disperse away from Christmas Island.

MASKED or BLUE-FACED BOOBY (Mouakena) *Sula dactylatra* Resident. Nests scattered among sparse or low vegetation, especially on the south-east peninsula. Ground nesting.

BROWN BOOBY (Kibui) *Sula leucogaster* Least common booby on Christmas Island. Nests on ground in small, widely scattered colonies.

GREAT FRIGATEBIRD (Eitei) *Fregata minor* Common resident. Main breeding colonies in central lagoon areas both on islets and on main island. Roosts in trees at places where they do not nest.

LEAST FRIGATEBIRD (Eitei) *Fregata ariel* Resident. Less common than Great Frigatebird. Breeds among dense saltbush scrub (*Suriana*) south of Isles Lagoon.

REEF HERON (Kaai or Matuku) *Demigretta sacra* Rare visitor. Sight rècords at ponds near Banana Village. Common resident in Central Gilberts.

MALLARD (Tiriwenei) *Anas platyrhynchos* Migrant, frequenting inland pools, mainly October to November. Numbers vary from year to year. Breeds in North America.

PINTAIL DUCK *Anas acuta* Regular migrant in small numbers, mainly September to November and again in January and February. Breeds in North America.

NORTHERN SHOVELLER (Tiriwenei) *Spatula clypeata* Migrant in small numbers during months of the northern winter. Breeds in North America.

GREATER SCAUP *Aythya marila* Rare winter migrant. Breeds in North America.

PACIFIC GOLDEN PLOVER (Kun) *Pluvialis dominica* Regular migrant, arriving September and remaining until May or June. Frequents inland pools and flats with dry scrub.

TURNSTONE (Kitiba) *Arenaria interpres* Migrant, flocks frequently up to twenty present from September to March or April on tidal flats and shores. Breeding grounds in Arctic.

BRISTLE-THIGHED CURLEW (Kewe) *Numenius tahitiensis* Migrant, present as individuals and small groups September to May or early June. Breeds on the tundra in Alaska.

WANDERING TATTLER (Kiriri) *Heteroscelus incanus* Migrant, mainly September to June although non-breeding individuals remain during northern summer. Commonest shore bird.

SANDERLING *Crocethia alba* Migrant in small numbers during northern winter. Breeds in Arctic.

RING-BILLED GULL *Larus delawarensis* Rare vagrant from North America.

CRESTED TERN (Karabara) *Thalasseus bergii* Common throughout year fishing over lagoon or on the shelf reef. Nesting appears to be confined to Cook Island.

SOOTY TERN (Kereekere) *Sterna fuscata* Huge colonies breed on the main island and on Cook Island. Twice yearly nesting peaks, in June and December. Most abundant bird of the Central Pacific. Pelagic outside nesting season.

SPECTACLED or GREY-BACKED TERN (Tarangongo) *Sterna lunata* Resident, breeding on islets in Manulu and Isles Lagoons and on tidal flats of main lagoon. Laying occurs late December to May.

COMMON or BROWN NODDY ,(Io) *Anous stolidus* Common resident, breeding on lagoon islets. Ground nesting in Christmas Island.

WHITE-CAPPED or BLACK NODDY (Mangkiri, Kunei or Takiri) *Anous minutus* Abundant, nesting in trees on lagoon islets. Seen in small flocks flying out to feed at sea.

BLACK-NAPED TERN (Kiakia) *Sterna sumatrana* Vagrant from the Tropical Western Pacific. Breeds in Central Gilberts.

BLUE-GREY NODDY *Procelsterna cerulea* Resident although individuals may leave between breeding periods. Laying occurs May to December. Nests on ground on lagoon islets. Probably the only oceanic bird which is significantly insectivorous (catching the marine water-strider, *Halobates*).

WHITE or FAIRY TERN (Matawa) *Gygis alba* Resident, breeding on lagoon islets May to November. No nest made and single egg incubated on bare branch of tree.

SCARLET-BREASTED LORAKEET or KUHL'S LORY (Kura) *Vini kuhlii* Probably introduced by early Polynesian voyagers from Rimitara in the Tubuai Islands. Nests on Fanning and Washington Islands. Introduced in recent years to Christmas Island but not yet established as breeding species.

CHRISTMAS ISLAND WARBLER (Bokikokiko) *Conopoderas aequinoctialis* The only resident indigenous landbird; endemic to Northern Line Islands. Nests in Ren trees March to June.

IBLIOGRAPHY

Those starred (★) have been used as sources, inter alia, in the compilation of this history.

Admiralty *Pacific Island Pilot*, London

★**Allen, P. S.** (1922) *Stewart's Handbook of the Pacific Islands*, Sydney, Australia

Anon (1848) *The Wreck of the Bremen Whaleship "Mozart"*, The *Friend*, October 77

Barnett, M. A. F. (1961) *Climatic features of the tropical Southwest Pacific*, N.Z. Met. Serv. Teach. Inf. Circ. 108

Beaglehole, J. C. (1934) *The Exploration of the Pacific*, London p. 357

★**Beaglehole, J. C.** (1974) *The Life of Captain James Cook*, A. & C. Black of London, England and Stanford University Press, California, U.S.A.

Bennett, F. D. (1840) *Narrative of a Whaling Voyage around the Globe, from year 1833 to 1836*, 2 vols. London

Benson, G. (1838) *Sketch of Christmas Island, with a chart of the island, Hawaiian Spectator* 1 (2): 64–68

Benson, G. (1857) *Christmas Island, The Friend*

Bryan, E. H. (1942) *American Polynesia and the Hawaiian Chain*, Tong Pub. Co., Honolulu

Bryan, E. H. (1953) *Checklist of Atolls*, Atoll. Res. Bull.

★**Buck, Peter H.** (1938) *Vikings of the Sunrise*, F. A. Stokes, New York

Burney, J. (1803) *A chronological history of the discoveries in the South Sea or Pacific Ocean*, London I: 179–185

Cameron, J. (1923) *John Cameron's Odyssey*, Macmillan, New York

Charles, H. C. (1960) *Fresh water resources*. Appendix 12 of report of the work of the Army element. Task Force Grapple. Vol. 2 War Office, London

★Chief Minister's Office Ministry of the Chief Minister, Tarawa, Gilbert Islands

Chock, A. K. and Hamilton, D. C. Jr. (1962) *Plants of Christmas Island*, Atoll. Res. Bull. 90: 1–7

Coffee, F. (1920) *Forty years on the Pacific*, New York, pp. 93, 173–174

★Cook, Capt. James and King, Capt. James (1784) *A Voyage To The Pacific Ocean*, Stockdale and Fielding, London

Crowther, W. E. L. H. (1939) *The development of the Guano trade from Hobart Town in the fifties and sixties*, Pap. Prec. R. Soc. Tasmania, 1938: 213–221

★Cyclopedia of Fiji (1907)

★Desbois, Fr. J. M. *Naililili*

Donagisio, W. (1952–3) Journal of the 1938 Line Islands expedition, *Elepaio*, 13: 22–25, 34–36, 43–44, 48–50, 60–62 and 66–69

Drauss, N. L. (1953) *Insects and other Invertebrae from Palmyra Atoll and Christmas Island*, Prec. Haw. Ent. Soc. 15(1): 217–220

Eaddy, P. A. (1943) *Neath swaying spars*, New Zealand

★Emory, K. P. (1934) *Archaeology of the Pacific Equatorial Islands*, Bishop Museum Bulletin 123

Fairfax-Ross, B. (1937) *Christmas Island* (Unpublished Report)

★Fiji Times Various dates

★Findlay, A. G. (1884) *A Directory for the Navigation of the S. Pacific Ocean*, 5th Ed. London

Fosberg, F. R. (1957) *Soils, vegetation and agriculture on coral atolls*, Prec. 8th Pac. Sci. Congr. (1953), IIIA: 1637–1647

Gallagher, M. D. (1960) *Bird notes from Christmas Island, Pacific Ocean*, Ibis. 102: 489–502

Gallagher, M. D. et al (1958) Bull. Christmas Island Nat. Hist. Sec. 1–5, 7–11

Gallagher, M. D., Hancox, J. W. et al (1959) *Vegetation on Christmas Island*, Bull. Christmas Island Nat. Hist. Sec. 6

★**Gatty, H.** (1943) *The Raft Book—Lore of the Sea and Sky*, George Grady Press, New York

Gerlach, J. C. (1955) *Report on an agricultural survey of Christmas Island*, Dept. Agric. New Zealand

Gessler, C. (1937) *The Dangerous Island*, London, pp. 39 and 47

Gilbert Islands Colony Annual Reports

Gutch, J. (1962) *Christmas Island, Geog. Mag.* 35(4): 181–189

Hague, J. D. (1862) *On phosphatic guano islands of the Pacific Ocean, AM. J. SCI.* 2nd Series 34 (101): 224–243

Harvey, T. (1860) *Notes of a voyage to the Pacific in H.M.S. Havanna, Naut. Mag.* 29. (6) (7) (8) (10) (11); 302–307, 358–361, 420–425, 521–525, 587–591

★**Hydrographic Dept.** Ministry of Defence, Taunton, Somerset, England

★**Hydrographic Office** *Sailing Directions for the Pacific Islands*, U.S. Navy Dept.

Ingram, W. M. (1937) *Cypraeidac from Christmas, Palmyra, Washington and Fanning Islands, The Nautilis* 51(1): 1–3

★**Jenkin, R. N. and Foale, M. A.** (1968) *An Investigation of the Coconut-growing Potential of Christmas Island*, Directorate of Overseas Surveys, England

King, J. E. (1955) *Annotated list of birds observed on Christmas Island, October to December, 1953*, Pac. Sci. 9(1): 42–48

★**Lands Office** Ministry of Local Government and Rural Development, Tarawa, Gilbert Islands

Lathbury, G. (1958) *Christmas Island, Elepaio*, 19(5): 30–31
Leembruggen, E. L. (1936) *Christmas Island* (Unpublished Report)
★Leibert, Miss K. (1969) *A Narrative History of Christmas Island* (Unpublished Thesis), Worcester College
★Lewis, David (1972) *We, the Navigators*, A. H. & A. W. Reed, Wellington, New Zealand
Lucette, M. (1851) *Rovings in the Pacific from 1837 to 1849 with a glance at California*, London, 2: 234–245
Maude, H. E. (1957) *Sovereignty over Christmas Island, Aust. Outlook*, 11(3): 31–37
★Maude, H. E. (1959) *Spanish Discoveries in the Central Pacific: a Study in Identification*, J. Polyn. Soc. 68(4): 284–326
Maude, H. E. (1961) *Post-Spanish discoveries in the central Pacific*, J. Polyn. Soc. 70(1): 67–111
McClery, F. E. (1959) *A Christmas Island climatological study*, Joint Task Force 7, Meteorological Center, Pearl Harbour, Honolulu
Meadows, D. J. (1963) *Visit to Christmas Island*. Tarawa. Gilbert Islands (Unpublished Report)
Ministry of Aviation (1958) *Operation Grapple*, London
Moss, F. J. (1889) *Through atolls and islands in the Great South Sea*, London, pp. 15 and 154–155
★Naval Intelligence Division *Geographical Handbook Series — Pacific Islands*, Vol. II, 1943
New Zealand Meteorological Office (1943) *The climate of the northern Line Islands*, Clim. Notes, C(11): 1–12
Northrop, J. (1962) *Geophysical observations on Christmas Island*, Atoll Res. Bull. 89: 1–2
★O'Reilly, P. (1958) *Imprints of the Fiji Catholic Mission, incl. the Loreto Press 1864–1954*

83

★Pacific Islands Monthly Magazine (various years) Sydney, Australia

Pacific Publications Pty. Ltd. (1959) *Pacific Islands Yearbook*, Sydney, Australia

Palmer, P. (1939) *Christmas Island* (Unpublished Report)

Palmer, P. (1943) *Christmas Island* (Unpublished Report)

★Philatelic Club of Sydney (1953) *Christmas Island and Its Postal History*

Pilsbry, H. A., Cooke, C. M. and Neal, M. C. (1928) *Land snails from Hawaii, Christmas Island and Samoa*, Bishop Mus. Bull. 47: 1–49

★Public Records Office Chancery Lane, London, England

Rougier, E. (1914) *Ile de Christmas, South Seas (Océanie)*, Brioude

Rougier, E. (1917) *Ile de Christmas*, Bull. Soc. Etudes Ocean, 1: 15–30

Rougier, E. (1925) *Travelling around Christmas Island*, Mid-Pacific 29: 865–870

★Royal Commonwealth Society Library, London, England

★Schreiber, R. W. and Ashmole, N. P. (1970) *Sea-bird Breeding Seasons on Christmas Island, Pacific Ocean*, Ibis 112: 363–394

Scott, J. (1841) *Christmas Island*, Naut. Mag. 1841: 589–590

★State Department Historical Office, Washington D.C., U.S.A.

Stoddart, D. R. (Ed). (1962) *Coral Islands*, Atoll Res. Bull. 88: 1–20

Tresillan, F. H. (1838) *Remarks on Christmas Island, Hawaiian Spectator*, 1: 241–247

★Western Pacific Archives Suva, Fiji

85

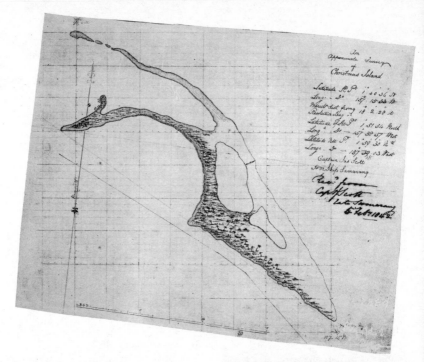

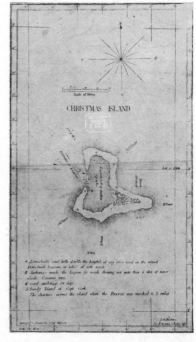

Above: *Captain Scott's map of Christmas Island drawn in 1842.*
Right: *Captain Benson's map dated 1837.*

Acknowledgements
The publishers gratefully acknowledge the following for providing the illustrations which are listed by page number, from top to bottom and left to right:

Cover: The Resolution|by Henry Roberts, Mitchell Library, Sydney, Australia; *Inside front and back cover*: Department of Geography, University of Durham; *i*: Mansell Collection; *ii*: British Library; Bishop Museum, Hawaii; *iii*: Mary Evans Picture Library; Mansell Collection; Mary Evans Picture Library; *iv*: Voyage to the Pacific 1776–80, Captain James Cook, 1784; Mary Evans Picture Library; *v*: P. D. Macdonald; Encyclopaedia of Fiji, 1907; *vi–vii*: The Gilbert Islands Government; James Brophy (2); *viii*: Central Office of Information, London; *ix*: James Brophy (2); The Gilbert Islands Government (4); *x*: James Brophy; *xi*: James Brophy (2); *xii–xiii*: James Brophy (3); *xiv*: Directorate of Overseas Surveys, London; *xv*: James Brophy (3); *xvi*: James Brophy (3); *88*: Hydrographic Department, Taunton, England (2).

The publishers are also grateful to the following: Elizabeth Bailey, Charlotte Odgers, Michael Rice and Co, Maurice Chandler, Clio Coles, Will Facey, Ay Lan Ng and Michèle Clarke.

88

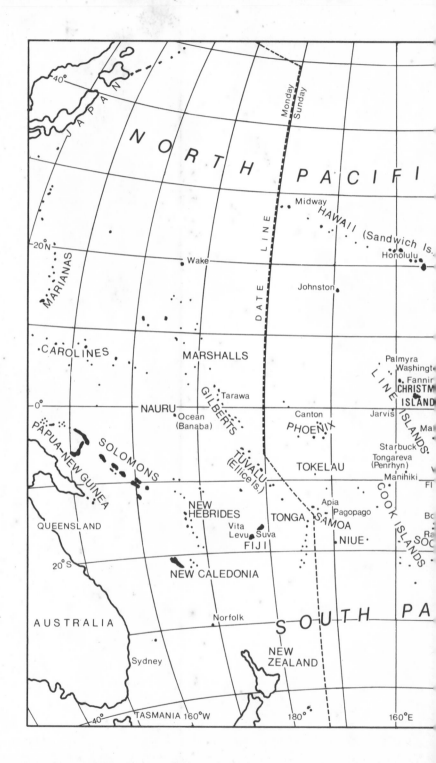